I0160999

Table of Content

About the Author

Author, Adriel Davis, was born and raised in Tallahassee, FL. He received a Bright Future scholarship to attend the University of Florida where he earned his bachelor's degree. As a college athlete playing basketball for the Florida Gators, Adriel assisted his team anyway that he could and also worked on the staff after he stopped playing basketball. He wanted more in his life after his college experience and decided to move to South Florida where he began writing "Pen to Paper." Shortly after his first publication, Adriel began working on "Sleepless Nights Endless Canvas." Adriel has a master's degree in athletic administration from Nova Southeastern University and a master's degree in business administration from Saint Leo University. In the summer of 2017 he completed his third master's degree at Florida International University. He is an author, an athlete, and a scholar whose plan is to continue to make a positive change each and every day.

Acknowledgement and Dedication

Sleepless Pen Endless Canvas would not be possible without my experiences in life and the many people who have confided in me over the years. I would also like to thank my family and friends for all their support and always believing in me. This book is dedicated to everyone that has touched my life and I hope this book will touch your life. I would also like to thank Neil Butcher for the book cover and Dr. Christine Keaney (editor) for their assistance in helping produce my book, "Sleepless Pen Endless Canvas."

911

Love came in the front door

I ran out the back door

911, please come to my rescue

Being chased by a killer

It's been stalking me for years

Preying on my fears

I am running full speed

I can't get caught

I can't stop running

Cause if I fall, it's all my fault

911, I need you to come get this killer

It caught me once and nearly took my life

I recovered and kept out of sight

You can only hide for so long

So I'm calling for some backup

Because I am tired of running and this isn't funny

911, I can't find any love here

Cause I don't want to embrace it

And to be honest I am not ready to face it

911

This is an emergency

A Love Poem without Love

It's like water with no well
A cause without an effect
A poem without love
Are just words on paper
A journey with no destination
So find love
Or let it find you
Don't hide
Because it's an amazing thing
It is what makes the birds sing
It is why the world turns
It's the burn you get
When you know you in love
Something special
A love poem without Love
It's no poem at all
Just a free fall
To hell
Being imprisoned
Just not jail
So find a way to love
Or allow yourself to be loved
Because in the end
Only angels travel above

Afraid of Fear

It's not you I fear

It's love I am afraid of

Afraid of giving you my heart

Watching you walk away with it

Unable to fight you as you walk away

Watching as every step you make takes my breath away

Afraid of fear

Because it lurks deep in my soul

Not allowing me to be loved

Preventing me from falling into love

Afraid of you

Fearful of me

Trying to complete the task

But fear has me not being me

Wanting to Love

But unable to learn

I guess I will sit here

Afraid of Fear

As the pain continues to burn

All I Want

What I want is not what I need

My relationship destroyed right before my eyes

You can't see my pain you didn't feel the lies

You never saw my trials and tribulations

All you want to do is put me on trial

Maybe I am not ready

Maybe I am afraid

Maybe I lost everything I had

Maybe I am still trying to find the pieces of me that I lost

Maybe you just like the others, false

All I want

Is not everything that I need

I want to find a foundation

Plant a seed

Nurture it

Watch it grow

This time, I want to find

Someone willing to intertwine it with our love

Cast a pray above

Release love

Let God handle the rest

All I want

Is pure unconditional love

Alone with my Thoughts

Many long nights

I tossed and turned

My thoughts burning

Like an uncontrolled blaze

Caging my fears

Stirring a desire that was bigger than me

Me not being able to see

Who I was supposed to become

To busy trying to fit into a place

I could never fit

Then I heard the words from the man above

Speaking of an unconditional love

That's beyond conventional

Many long nights

I tossed and turned

Until I learned to listen to my heart

And the man above

Now I know love

Along This Ride

Swallow my pride

How can I when you weren't on my ride

You have no idea what my joys were

Or what my grieves came from

Don't discount my fears

I endured pain for years

I shed so many tears

That I drowned myself in them

So don't sit and judge

When you all you can see is my cover

You afraid to read my story

Due to it being easier to cast a stone

Than to lend a hand

That is the problem with mankind

They forgot how to be kind

How can I open my mind?

When my heart needs a kind touch

All I get is a knife to the gut

Slowly bleeding

While swallowing my pride

Yet, you want to cast judgment

Because you afraid to join me on this ride

As I Sit and Contemplate My Next Direction

As I sit and contemplate my next direction

Remorseful of all the misdirection I caused

Telling myself that I can't change the past

But scared from all the pain I caused

And broken from all the pain I endured

So as I embark on this new journey

Wishing it wasn't alone

I tell myself it's better to travel alone

Still, it bothers me that

My other half is aloft

One day we will unite

Face to face

Armed with nothing but faith, loyalty and the truth

As I air out these thoughts

I am caught up

In who I was

Then immediately I realize

It's more important that I focus on

Who I am becoming

Remorseful

Never regretful of this misguided journey

As I Sit and Look at Your Smile

As I sit and look at your smile

It reminds me of such a calm and peaceful time

I know you're not mine

But you're always on my mind

The joy you bring

The magic of your eyes

The touch of your soul

Somehow filling the gaps and makes me whole

I have no clue of where this journey will lead

But when I look in your eyes

I can see peace love and joy

And with that, this journey is well worth the ride

As I sit back and look in your eyes

As I Sit and Wait

As I sit and wait
I feel like time has frozen
And I want this moment to never end
I know it's more than a dream
That I wish I can never awaken from
Some say love is elusive
At times I agree
But I can still hold on to the pieces
Of life that has shown me the power of love
If this is just a dream
I'll cherish its memories forever
If this is real life
Than every trial and tribulation
That lead me here
Was worth every tear I shed
And every time I question
If I'll ever find love
As I sit and wait
To see if this is a dream

As the Angels Cry

When my tears are shed

My soul is exposed

Unaware that anyone heard my cries

I floated along life

Like water along a stream

Embrace life, but not dreams

Then the skies begin to open

Just as my eyes were beginning to close

Behold my son

I am the light

Your salvation

Seek me

Before seeking the air, you breathe

I heard your cries

And gave you a blessing for every tear you shed

Now open your heart

And I shall protect your soul

Be kind to those

Whom are not kind to you

And I shall keep you whole

As my Angels cry

Your blessings will never die

You are in my care

I will never give you more than you can be

Beautiful Lies, Ugly Truths

Beautiful lies

Ugly truths

You want to hear both

But can't handle the two

One is sweet, yet cuts like a knife

One if you hear it, you want out of my life

Stuck between a rock and a hard place

When face to face

With beautiful lies

And ugly truths

Which do you want?

Turned away

By the ambiguity of the situation

Do you want to hear sweet meaningless words?

Or coldhearted truth?

Establishing a foundation of one

Can you handle it through and through?

Beautiful lies

Face the ugly truth

I say I love you

Is it a beautiful lie?

Or the ugly truth?

Beauty and the Beast

She was beauty
And I had become a beast
One that pushed her away
One that had developed an ugly soul
She refused to accept me as a beast
She seen past those scars, past the darkness
She wanted to be my light
But she knew I had to see it in myself first
She was beauty and I was a beast
Frightening anyone who dare love me
She only wanted to love me
And open my eyes
She could tell I had been beaten up by lies
She could see what lies beneath
But she wanted to see me soar
So she opened up my heart
And let love pour
She was beauty
And I was a beast
Trying to be what she could see
That I couldn't see in myself

Beautiful Monster

You show your beauty on the outside
As if it will last
But outside beauty fades
When the inside last
Beauty from the inside will always seep out
Beauty from the outside will at some point rear an ugly head
You beautiful monster
That is what you are
Looking good from the outside
You think will get you far
But that little monster inside
Is who you really are
Beautiful monster
Your looks will soon fade
Right along with your friends
Disappearing like your age
Learn to be beautiful from the inside out
And cure yourself of that monster
Before it finds its' way out
Surfacing your true colors
That you hide so well
Beautiful monsters
Eventually, live in hell

Behind These Eyes

Behind these eyes

Is a man ready to hold your hand

Behind these eyes

Is a man tired of hearing the same song

Behind these eyes

Is a man tired of being judged by the things he did wrong

Behind these eyes

Is a man who is there for you during your ups and downs

Behind these eyes

Is a man who is ready

Behind these eyes

Is a man ready to write a new song

Behind these eyes

Is a man who wants you to be the paper, and be your pen

Behind these eyes

Is a man who wants to be the melody to your song

Behind these eyes

Is a man

Who just wants to your man

Behind these eyes

Is a man with his arms out

Ready to embrace you

Upon your arrival

Behind these eyes

Lies a love like no other

Behind These Eyes Part II

Behind these eyes lies a man

Trying to do better

Driving myself insane

A man who hides his pain

A man who is everyone's shoulder, never receiving the same

Living my life yet feeling like I am in a video game

Behind these eyes is where I shed my tears

Keeping them away so you never see my fears

Writing on this pad to keep my sanity

The weight on my shoulders is heavier than it looks

That is why I tell this story and call it a book

Behind these eyes

Lies secrets you may never know

You may read about it

Yet you never know

What lies behind these eyes

Best Friend

This is to you,
I guess before you were wondering who?
This is to you, my best friend

The one that makes me smile,
The one that makes me laugh

I guess before you didn't know,
But you are my best friend

The way I feel when we chill,
The way life without you has no thrill

So to my best friend,
One thing I can ensure you, is that this is real
I want you to know
I Love you, my best friend

Between the Lines

I was whole, but it wasn't until I was broken

That the light was able to shine

To illuminate and allow me to shine

The pieces are exposed

Much like my soul

When I was whole I was hot

But I was cold when I became broken

These are the words of my diary

So read with care

I dare you to walk into my world

And leave being the same

I am trained to be numb

Because life has beaten me up

I want to be human for you

But I feel like an alien on earth

Touch me

So I can know what it feels to be human again

I was once whole

But all these broken pieces

Show the light of my soul

The question is can you read the script

Amongst these broken lines

The pieces are exposed

I am here if you want to be mine

Just read between the lines

Bigger than Me

Have you not realized our love is bigger than me

It's more than either one of us can see

You can dwell

But dwelling wrong has our relationship in hell

Stop feeding the bad

And start nursing the good

We in this together whether you weather the storm

Or leave me in the cold

I'll hold us together

I am proud of us

Have you not realized our love is bigger than me

Just open your heart and you will see

It's more than either one of us can see

Bitch, Fuck You

Words, can't explain the pain in this letter

But, calling you a bitch somehow makes it better

I was there for you, during the stormy weather

Now I am saying Fuck You

Cause you are the worse kind of weather

Consumed by emotions

That is directed towards you

If I only had one person to call a Bitch

It would for sure be you

I was your rock

When you needed someone strong

But just like a rock

You threw me away

Now my days are amassed with pain

Directed towards you

Because I bought into your games

Ashamed of myself

For believing in you

I guess the saying is true

That Love is a Bitch

And that Bitch was you

So here is my farewell

For you to fuck Off

Bitch, Go Away

Bitch, and I use that word with fury

When the thought of you comes to mind, I get weary

I hate you bitch, and that is me being modest

Go away

Don't speak another word

Look at my fingers

Yea, bitch that is a bird

You remind me of a fucking turd

Nah, more like shit

To think I once loved you trick

Bitch, go away

Far, far, far away

Deeper than the lowest jail

Bitch, go away

The best place would be hell

I lent you my heart

You sold it for parts

Bitch, go away

I packed your shit in a shopping cart

Bitch, just go away

Bitches on a String

Bitches on a string

Hanging around, looking for a ring

Mimicking all these love songs as if they can sing

They all sound alike

They don't even ask if relationships are your thing

Bitches on a string

Dancing to every move you make

Yet, won't play their part

While seeking a leading role

Digging in your pockets

Like it's a pot of gold

Bitches on a string

Looking like puppets in a show

If they were there for you, they would never go

They want to play the role like Halle

But they are barely seen

Bitches dance on a string

With hopes of a ring

You will never find the man of your dreams

If you remain

The bitch on a string

Blind Side of Love

Some Love without being in love
Some go to the beach, and never see the ocean
Some meet a person and think they're the potion
The Blind Side of Love
Is the learn, to live and to dream
Let your feeling flow like the river
Imagine the rainbow
Even when it is not raining
The Blind Side of Love
Could be what you're gaining
Never knowing where it came from
Or when it began
Just grab love and hold its hand
The term love is blind
Could be the reason why it passes us by
But the funny thing is
It is there; we just never really try
To engage ourselves
In the things we think are love
Stop being blink
And open your eyes
Because in every blink of the eye
Time flies
So don't be deceived by these blind eyes
They are soft and kind
They are one of kind
Blind Side of Love
Be mine

Blood, Sweat, and Tears

Blood, Sweat, and Tears
Are overshadowed
By Love, Perception, and Fears
Let me in your heart
And poison you will taste
Like venom injected directly into your face
Blood, Sweat, and Tears
Have abused me over the years
This blood I shed
Is fire red
Dripping from my soul until it was dead
Those beads of sweat
I shall never forget
They lead to my anxiety
That I couldn't shake
Caused my heart to fall asleep
Never to reawaken
Those tears
Were not of joy
They were of pain
Expose my heart
Only to be left in shame
Blood, Sweat, and Tears
Of a well-worn man
These callused hands
Will help me understand
Why this

Blood, Sweat, and Tears

Have shaped a man

Who

Was exposed

To so many fears

Throughout his years

That has drained him

Of all his

Blood, Sweat, and Tears

Bloodshot Eyes

Bloodshot
Eyes bloodshot red
Dark as crimson tide
Sipping on this whiskey
Reflecting on my lies
How did I get here?
I never meant to hurt anyone
As I chase the bottom of the glass
As if the solution is at the end
Fading in and out
Trying to drown my sorrow
This whiskey won't kick in
It's kicking my ass
Telling me everything I didn't do
Waking up all the voices in my mind
Yelling at me, telling me the truth
Replaying all the recorded lies
Trying to tell me to be a better man
Bloodshot
Eyes bloodshot red
Wish this whiskey would kick in
So I can drown my sorrows
Chasing the bottom of this glass
Knowing it won't numb the pain
So I'll keep sipping
Hoping it will fade
With the sins of my past
Bloodshot eyes

Breaking the Law of Love

When you feeling imprisoned

And need someone to break you out

Let me pull you through

I will break all the laws

Just to be next to you

Breaking the Laws

To get you what you need

Any Law of Love

I will risk getting caught

Just to steal you away from imprisonment

I will never stop breaking the Laws of Love for you

I will keep running from the Laws of Love

I will speed so fast; they will never catch us

I will run away with you

So that you can feel love

Even if it means breaking the Laws of Love

And running away from my own love

Just to break the Laws of Love with you

Broken Silence

When it works

It works well

If I love you

Must I tell?

Broke by the strong holds of my past

I open my heart

How long will it last?

Show me a reason

To need love in my life

And I show you a soul

That is as dark as coal

Not sure where to go

Or even who to call

My role is to be the shoulder for all

But when I am weak

Or I just can't sleep

Who is there to console me when I weep?

The burdens get heavier

The road a lot longer

I keep asking myself

Can I get any stronger?

The world on my shoulder

And my back is near broken

My cry for help

And no one seems to notice

My heart is adrift

And my soul is becoming stiff

Because my role

As a hero is starting to shift

Nowhere to go

So I seek out a cage

Where I can remain closed

And suppress and disengage

There I will be fine

As I close doors

And begin

To hide

As I fade away

My heart, my soul, and mind.

Can't Turn Back

I keep looking back
But I can't turn back
What's done is done
But the damage still exists
My heart has become tighter than my fist
I took the risk
Of loving once in my life
It gave me heartache and strife
Now you asking me to let go of this fight
Yes, I see love and its right in your eyes
The mirror of those eyes reflects lies
Not of ones you told
But of ones I hold
In from the weight
I dragged along the way
I'm telling you I love you
Is that enough for you to stay?
I can't turn back
Nor change the root of my heart
But if you plant a good seed
It can outgrow the weeds
That has torn my heart to shreds
I can't turn back
I am trying to look ahead
Give me time to keep moving your way
If it's not too much
I would love for you to stay
Because I can't turn back

Caramel Skin

She has caramel skin

With a caramel taste

Every time I close my eyes all I can see is her face

Wondering when I can combine her smell with her taste

When every love song is meant for her

Her aura draws me near

She pushes me away, because of fear

Caramel skin, I love your touch

If I say I love you, have I said too much?

Your taste is sensational

Your body is amazing

You set fire to my heart and now it is blazing

Caramel skin

You are melting me away

I will be your chocolate

And I want to mix with your caramel

Each and Every day

Come Back Home

I know you're gone

But why did you leave

I use to be close

Now I wear my heart on my sleeve

Ready to shed a tear

When thoughts of you are near

Being alone has become my biggest fear

Now when I go to war

I don't have you by my side

I looked in my rearview

Cause pieces of me have died

Come back home

To help me face this world

Come back home

Everything

Everywhere

Is a reminder of you

I want to know, what did I do?

That made you depart

If you return

I will hand you my heart

Come back home

That is where it starts

Commitment Issues

In love with the moment
Each moment a loss
Lost in this moment
Just because I can't commit
The real issue is my past
It poisons my system
Nearly killed my ass
Commitment issues
I want your heart
But I know you won't wait forever
I see us at the altar, side by side
Holding each other's hands
The seed was planted
And it grew into pain
Commitment issues
Have corrupted my brain
Withered away my soul
Commitment issues
You left me in pieces
Now, how do I become whole?

Connected

Link by Link
Piece by Piece
I will rebuild
This troubled soul
Searching for answers
In hopes of once again
Becoming whole
Connected at one point to every piece of the puzzle
Hurt so bad I put love in a muzzle
Because it bit me bad
Forcing me to turmoil
Stuck on sad
Reconnect me
Please
Because I am walking on my knees
The pain is aching
Something I can't shake
If this is a nightmare
Then it's time to wake
Connect me to peace
Before I have no pieces remaining
I want to reconnect
So I know I am gaining
A new connection
Hopefully with love
Since it was the cause
For giving me all this pain
Connect me, please
With Love once again

Crazy Love

Crazy is what

What crazy does

And some crazy people

Are crazy in love

Crazy love; is it stalking?

Is it finding someone and never letting them go?

Crazy Love

How do you define it?

If you have it, do others mind it?

Are you crazy if you're in love?

Does love make you crazy?

If love is crazy

Why are so many people after it?

Crazy is what

What crazy does

We all must be crazy

Cause we seek that Crazy Love

Crumbling Walls

These four walls
Have me caged in
It's my fault
I built myself in them
They were supposed to protect me
So I couldn't let you in
Allowing you to torment my soul
And criticize my heart
These walls have only crippled my well-being
Until I can't even see
Beautiful things surround me
I can feel them in my bones
If you have the power
Please disengage these walls
Breakthrough
Until they crumble at our feet
Then embrace
And together we will be

Crying in the Rain

Sometimes we hold on to things so hard

Even within ourselves

Then we decide to let go because it has all falling apart

We must release the choke hold

Allowing things to breathe, before we kill it

Crying in the Rain so that no one can see my tears

Holding on to my heart, because of the things I fear

Then when I let it go, there was nothing to fear

Because there was nothing there anymore

I held on to it for too long

I have been to hell and back

Looking to enter Heaven and never leave

Crying in the rain

Because I am ashamed

Hiding the tears amongst the rain

I feel safer when

Crying in the Rain

Cupid

Touched by a soul

That didn't belong to me

Holding to what was

Because it no longer is

Sitting and looking in a mirror

While I shed these tears

Paralyzed by Cupid

Because he missed my heart

And hit my spine

Crippled not only by my legs

But my heart is numb

I see Valentine's Day

And I run

Love me every day not

Just on this one

Touched by your soul

Even though he has the key

If he ever loses you

Please find me

Yearning for your soul

Even though it doesn't belong to me

Happy Valentine's Day

It's your heart I seek

Cupid is Near

Is that who you fear?

Don't sing a song that doesn't make music

Don't live without Love

Because a love poem without love

Is just words on a paper

Dancing While I Burn

Dancing with the Devil

He has become my friend

He replaced my heart after its heavenly end

I had no place to go

So heartbreak became my deadly sin

In my mind it was win-win

No longer feeling the emotional toll of love

No longer feeling the rain from Heaven above

Those drops of rain were my tears

Burning me alive

Creating more fears

So I heard a song

That led me to a place

That had a catchy beat

I got on the dance floor

And started making my moves

All I saw was the trail of a broken heart

That I had somehow consumed

Dancing with the Devil

Now I am stuck in this cocoon

While dancing with the Devil

In this deadly womb

Dancing with the Devil

Dancing with the Devil

Cause he knows my song

He listened when those girls did me wrong

Dancing with the devil

Because he knows my beat

Destined for hell

Cause my anger won't sleep

Hell is a not a worry

I have been dead for years

Look in my chest

No heart in their lives

Dancing with the Devil

Since he knows me well

I accept my death and my trip to hell

Dancing with Devil

Cause cupid is a lie

I would poison his darts

Hope that he shoots himself and die

Dancing with the devil

Since he knows my beat

My heart is dead

So hell is where she sleep

Dark Clouds

Dark Clouds surround me every day

I want to surrender

I am no quitter

When did this start?

When did I get lost?

Love is here

Love is there

I refuse to allow love

To consume once again

Dark Clouds surround

So that I can no longer feel the pleasure of love

I rather sit in the foxhole alone

Than to have my heart blown

To pieces and left for dead

My dark clouds

Are alive

While love is dead

Darkness Lurks

The pain of the past

I thought I had outrun

But I wake up in cold sweat

And that is no fun

Dreams merge into Nightmares

Fairytales disappear like sunlight

The pain of the past

Haunts me as if it's stuck in the future

And I am stuck in overdrive with it moving right at me

I can't hide; I can't dodge it

It's lodged in my heart

Flows through my veins

It's a sick poison

That is driving me insane

The pain of my past

Grant me one wish

That all the pain you have caused

Will one day lead to a life of pleasure

At the rate that I am going, I will never make it out of this cold stormy weather

My skin is hard like leather

My heart is soft like flesh

The pain of my past prevents me from getting rest

Please let me be free

So my heart can see once again

If not, watch as my soul

Blows away in the wind

Daydreaming

They told me I was daydreaming

That I needed to date reality

They just didn't know who I was

I had a buzz about me that had a fight

When others were sleep at night

I was planning and plotting

Dropping to my knees

Saying Lord please

Guide me

Protect me

Now during the day my dreams are real

At night we plotting for even more

They locked doors

Shut me out

But you should have never counted me out

I am in a fight

But I have God in my corner

They told me I was daydreaming

When I was actually just living God's plan

My life will always be in his hands

Day 2 Day

Each day I wake up

You are on my mind

You are one of a kind

I just wish you could be mine

I reach out

But you are just out of reach

I kneel to pray

Asking for the day that you will be mine

I shed tears of fear

Cause I feel you will never be here

I want you near my heart

Close to my soul

I feel cold without

You in my life

This is my cry

This is my plea

Let's drop the I and make this a We

Me and you

Without you my dreams

Becomes nightmares

My happiness

Becomes sadness

Accept my offer

And the reward

Is the World

Deadly Sins of Love

The deadliest sin of them all
Has fallen into my life
I reopen my heart
Only to have it crushed again
What is the purpose of trying again
When I can't win at this game of love
Beaten worse than the first time I fell
I know this isn't Heaven; this has to be hell
Destined for a torn heart
They could have warned me from the start
Trying to repair my wounds
When fear and pain is all my body has consumed
Trying to regurgitate this bad taste
But I can't when I am losing this race
Meet me at the finish line
Is all I hear
Sorry I ran out of gas my dear
Deadly Sins of Love
Has become my grim reaper
If I find true love
I promise to keep her
Until then
Deadly sins of love
Haunt my every thought
I am running, but
Praying and wishing
I get caught

By the Heavenly Hands of Love

So she may wash away

These deadly sins of Love

Deliciously Beautiful

Deliciously beautiful

Sadly, mistaken

I want you

I feel you're taken

Maybe not by another being

But when I look in your eyes

It's trouble I am seeing

The double edge sword

Has cut us both deep

I still toss and turn

Only wish I could sleep

The past is my tool to heal

The present is real

The future is my dream

It seems so far fetched

But Love is deliciously beautiful

Or am I sadly mistaken?

If I think it won't hurt

If we see eye to eye

This just might work

Take care,

Of the seconds

Cherish the minutes

Embrace the hour

Make it through the days

Hold hands together

And let's find a way

To make this deliciously beautiful

Without being sadly mistaken

Destiny

After looking into your eyes

I was never the same

I saw myself and you

Like a picture in a frame

Destiny had finally met chance

All doubts and worries

Put to rest

Handed you my heart

Expecting the best

Attracted to your heart

But in love with your soul

Feeling complete

Fulfilled and whole

No other feeling could

Match this sensation

You are my all

Your soul sings like The Temptations

Not knowing where I was

But finally where I am going

Kissing your lips

Is like fairy tale

Except I am the book

And you are the words

So please put your words all over my soul

The first time we touch

My life finally became whole

Distorted Images

The man in the mirror

That you once saw

Does not abide by the same laws from before

He has evolved

Answered his calling

He quit stalling

Now I am sure

As you stare at this person

All the pain

All the tears

You blame them for what has become

But if you stuck in the past

Who is really dumb?

Trust what you may

But I have grown to find brighter days

You shattered my mirror once before

Leaving me a distorted image of myself

Questioning where I had been

Afraid of where I was going

Until I learned to step away from the mirror

And stop running from my shadow

Sunset beauty

Moonlight mood

Following my dreams

As you remain locked

In that dark room

D>O>A

Dead on Arrival

That is how I will be delivered

Cold, emotionless, and lifeless

So do not be excited

Because this is no gift

It's a blessing; dressed in a curse

Wearing black and red

With a halo above

Shed away the layers

And start to feed me new life

Enrich my blood

With your soothing words

Let your touch embrace my wounds

As they nurture them back to heal

DOA

That is my only delivery way

If you want a better half

This is how we play

The damage is done

The story is written

I was bit by my love

The kind that was sickened

So remove this venomous venom

So I can regain my strength

Time is not a factor

Dead on Arrival

That is my biggest detractor

Don't ? the Man

Don't ? me

Because you fear what you can't see

Don't ? my talent

Because I am not famous yet?

Don't ? my vision

Because you can't see what I see

Don't ? my focus

Because you're not as focused as me

Don't ? the man in the mirror

Because his life is becoming much clearer

Don't ? the work ethic of these hands

Because you don't ? the man

Don't Look Back

Before me, there was you and him
And before the end of this story
It will be me and you
Just relax and let go
He is gone, and so is the past
Why live in the past
When it's clear, it will never last
You have to let go
And can finally not look back
See what is in front
And move towards the light
Because the only one shining
Is the one you don't want to see
It is finally that time, for you to be free
Let me stand beside you
Let me stand behind you
So that you have a shoulder
And someone to catch you if you fall
As the days pass, let the past pass with them
And write a new story
With a better ending than
The one from your past

Emptiness

Searching to be fulfilled

But all I am left is with emptiness

Pouring my soul into others

Until there is nothing left of me

Trying to revive my heart

But death is all it sees

Trying to fill my soul

But seems only to be filled with darkness

Waiting in the dark

For some type of light

Praying for Love each and every night

Empty and afraid

Scared and enraged

I want to remove this emptiness

Someday be engaged

What have I done?

To be so unlucky

This search for love

Has left me secluded

Emptiness laced with grief

I am a lonely heart

And Emptiness

Is all I meet

End of Me

When the end of me is here
I will only be words on paper
A memory to brighten your day
An afterthought to some
As I roam this world a free spirit
Seeking to touch others even when I am no longer here
Something when wrong
A missed conversation
A kiss that never connected
A heart that never fully healed
Now I am sitting here heart like steel
When the only thing that I have ever stolen are hearts
My heart has rubbed against so many rocks
That it has no print
To leave an impression on anyone
End of Me
You know not about me
Where I been
Where I am going

Enlightened Love

Enlighten me

On what makes you smile

Enlighten me

On what heighten your senses

Let me be enlightened

By someone so bright

Add Love

Remove the fight

Unless it's fighting for you

That I will do

Enlighten me

So I can enlighten you

Bliss is near

Fear no longer exists

Enlightened by your touch

I don't need much else

Just your tender loving care

Enlighten me

So this feeling

We can share

In

Enlightened Love

Fading Pictures

They told me to take a picture

Because it will last longer

Well what about the people in the photos

How long will they last?

Are they there to just take until you are left with your last?

Fake people

Fade like fading pictures

They may last in that picture forever

But in your life, they may last never

Fading away

Just as ashes in wind

As we glance into our past

Looking at photos of the past

The memories and the photo may last forever

But the people in them may slowly

Fade away

Fate and Destiny

Torn away way too soon

Our love once stood out like the moon

We had the right chemistry

But the wrong timing

A ticking bomb

Ready to explode

We explore the world

Yet, never explored one another

We were so in tune

Now, we are like a scratched record

Recording each other wrongs

Too afraid to focus on our rights

Now we are staring at the end

But neither of us wants to see it end

So let fate and destiny meet

And let the chemistry and timing

Stand at our feet

I love you and I won't allow us

To feel this defeat

Our love will stand out like the moon

Fear of Success

Am I afraid?

Success is right around the corner

Less than 24 hours away

From making it

So why haven't I made a move

Have I lost my desire, my groove?

How did I get to this point?

Where do I go?

Take a step back

Look at the person in the mirror

He needs to realize

He is the THRILLER

The card dealer

And fear of success

Can be overcome

Nonetheless

Just accept that you are the best

Fickle Past

To mend your broken heart is to suffer

Like fixing your self-inflicted wound

To find the pleasure in the pain of the suffering

Now that is the true meaning of living

To open your heart after it has been damaged

Is like looking down the barrel of a gun already fired

Now if love is the answer

Then I would rather not know the question

Shared memories of my past

Pierce my soul like hollow-tip bullets

Reminding me of what has caused these murky feelings

Ask God for some type of healing

Suffer no more as the words read

But planted in the ground are poisonous seeds

Fearful of what may sprout

I have managed to hurt myself with self-doubt

Picking up the pieces of all this broken glass

Looking in this broken mirror

Cutting myself with memories of my past

Seeking the fountain of purity

So I can cleanse my soul

These tragic memories

For some reason refuse to unleash their hold

They fickle and it keeps my heart cold

Finally, Free

Finally, Free
When I was never in jail
I let my mind imprison me
Forced myself to live in Hell
Trying to get parole
And they didn't set me any bail
Finally, Free
Cause I told my heartache to swim in gasoline then take a trip to Hell
Finally, Free
I didn't realize the whole time I had the key
Blind, lost, and so confused
I was my own enemy
Treating myself like a fool
Finally, Free
No longer in a maze
Shook the devil
Now dancing with God
It was a battle
Boy was it hard
Finally, free
As you can see
Ready to love
Cause my heart is finally free

Fire

The genuine aspect of my heart

Is overshadowed by my pain

Overwhelmed with heartbreak

That moving on makes me feels nearly insane

Caught between what I want and what I need

My heart is covered in darkness, intertwined with weeds

Trying to open up

Just increases the pain

I know if I let go, I'll have more to gain

My heart and my mind refuse to meet

So I toss and turn, wish for sleep

Dreams swarm me like a ghost in the night

I want something more

It just doesn't seem in my sight

I fight with this demon

That is as close as my shadow

I want love, but I can't win that battle

Crossed between fear and desire

I won't give my all until

She sets my soul and heart on fire

Flat Lined Love

I have travelled this road for many years

Seek, searching, yearning, shedding tears

I am near the end of the road

It seems like this path will lead to a dead end

I am dancing to a beat

But I am missing the song

I am so hurt; I can't even explain what is wrong

Time has been passing me by so fast

I have this feeling that I refuse to let go

Even though I can't share it

I will hold on to it

Bare it

This aching pain

Has me claustrophobic

Trapped in my misery

Fearing that I'll remain on this road alone

Wish I could find my way back home

Maybe my love got lost in translation

And my heart has lost its beat

I might as well flat line

Because my heart and soul have become comatose

Into a deep dark sleep

Forever in Love

You touched my lips
Like fingers to a piano
Playing music to my heart
Until the song began to replay
You sang melodies to my soul
To clog up the holes
You anointed my heart
With love
So intense, the cold began to melt
You were my shoulder
Cause you heard my cry for help
As the tune goes on
I become stronger and stronger
Dancing to music you gave my heart
I never want this feeling to depart
Join me as we raise our voices in the rain
The purity of our hearts washes away the pain
Let us rejoice in the eyes of a new day
Join with my hands
And let's find a way
To embrace this feeling of bliss
I feel in love
Without a kiss
It was the music of your soul
That produced this new mode
The loving warmth
Has eliminated the cold

You touched my lips

Like fingers to a piano

You are the most amazing thing

Forever in love

This one will never be dismantled

Forever Words

You ask about my words

But you should be concerned about my life

I live in today

But I am not promised tomorrow

So I write these words

So that once I die

My words can live on

They will allow me to forever

Read my words

Embrace my story

They will allow you to touch my soul

Each word is a piece of me

Poured from my heart

Written with the ink of my soul

Forever written in your mind

Transferred to heart

To spread to the next person

Touching and joining

Each poem a story of my life

A story carried on by you

So as long as you keep reading

I will always be a part of you

So accept my life

One day it will become death

But my words will live on

Forever

Forgive but Can't Forget

I can forgive

I just can't forget

As I sit here

Knowing things don't always go as planned

Know I was good man, just wish I was a better man

My watches are right, but the timing was always off

Trying to sing a song, knowing the lyrics are wrong

I can forgive

I just can't forget

Your touch, your smile or your glow

You just as much the blame

And I know you don't want this anymore

Everything was right

But everything was wrong

So I'll write this poem

As if it was just another song

I can forgive

I just can't forget

Frienemies

I stopped wishing and started acting

Acting like the person I am

Gave up on the person you wanted me to be

Opened my eyes, so that I can learn to be free

Pulled away from all the critics

Allowed their words to motivate my moves

Had to step my swag up

And just do what it do

Learned to think two steps ahead

Protect my heart as if I was the FEDs

Part of me may be broken

But by no means am I broke

I take it, different people

Different strokes

Some of you think you know

Some you know better than you think

Just remember that things can

Change in just one blink

Slip Slip Slip

But who's going to fall?

Will it be the people you call your friends

Or the ones who you assume is your enemy

I guess I will call them what they are

My Frienemies!

Fuck, Shit, Damn

Fuck, Shit, Damn

I got myself in a jam

I fell in love

And in public holding her hand

When did this happen

What do I do?

I like her

But loving her, I can't do

Fuck, Shit, Damn

I don't want to hurt her bad

But I refuse to walk around and be sad

Fuck

Fuck

Fuck

She in love

Shit

Shit

Shit

All I wanted to do was hit

Damn

Damn

Damn

How the hell do I get out this jam?

Fuck, Shit, Damn

Get Away, Run Away

Slapped

Punched

Physical and mentally abused

Scars so deep you can still see the wounds

Torn from all things my heart adored

Tried to re-love, but got bored

Heart heavy, just like stone

Throwing rocks at my glass home

Shielded from love

Immune to pain

Searching for my heart

No progress has been made

Has the Reaper of love

Killed those hopes and dreams

Has my heart seeped out all its blood?

Like water down a stream

Let me be

Cause things can only get worse if you enter this home

You will freeze to death

From the cold of my soul

Enter at your own risk

Warning labels are posted

And my soul is haunted

By the pain and scars of the past

If you're smart

You would run fast

Not towards me

But away from me

Far Far Far away from me

Ghostly Tears

Stomach turning

Heart is burning

For a break

From it all

I carry the weight of the world

And my back is beginning to get weak

It's so bad

I no longer sleep

Afraid to enjoy the simple pleasures

I am in the storm, but it's hard to bare the weather

My skin once tough

Like that of a gator

No longer myself

Because I am fading away

Find a place with peace of mind

I will repay you

By asking you to be mine

As my stomach turns

And my mouth is dry

I just have one question

Do you hear my cry?

Giving up my Heart

Dear heart

Please let go

I have to give you away

Before you rot away

You have been locked in a box

It's time to breath

You can't allow her to leave

Give her your heart

Take that risk

You felt love with just that first kiss

Give love, receive love

Embrace love, enjoy love

Give up your heart

It may come back bruised

But keep it in the box

In the end, we all will lose

Give up your heart

Good Intention, Bad Results

My good intentions are coated in gold

My bad results damage my soul

Heart remains open, only because it's broken

Good intentions

Lead by a good heart

Bad result

Puts my kindness at a halt

Open me up and see my good

I wish I wish you would

Overwhelmed with bad result

With only good intention

If this is my life

What does it mean?

The pain in my heart

Is exposed like a ravine

Good Intention

Bad Results

I wish I had the power to put this to a halt

Bring only good intentions with good results

Guest in My Own Home

It's hard to be me, but it's even harder to prove you wrong

I'll use those doubts to become stronger

I hate feeling like a guest in my own home

It's hard to be in love

Much easier to run

I hear all the words when a love song comes on

But how do you respond when you're grown

But ain't finishing growing

Living in love

Sinning as friends

In the end, we will never win

I am becoming a better man

Forgive me for my mistakes

One day I'll be returning home

Right now I just feel like a guest

In my own home

Half Empty Cup

My cup half empty

My life slightly murky

I am hurt

But is speaking of it isn't worth it

Torn, worn and badly bruised

Steady walking

No longer can I cruise

Along this road

Trying to regain the strength

That once made me a man

I am trying to start over

The best way I can

My cup half empty

And nowhere to fill it up

Looking down,

There is a slow leak in my cup

Who really cares?

As the life of me flows to the ground

Will I be missed?

Will anyone miss me when I am no longer around?

Staggered and abused

By lies and betrayal

My heart is weak

But one thing is for sure

It won't fail

Opening my eyes to brighter days

Hungry for change

As my cup remains half empty

And the days pass me by

I guess the only way to fill this cup

Is with the tears I cry

Harder Times

Harder times
Are fine
I have it in my mind
That failure is something I am not tailored for
I want more
And if you don't need to give it to me
I am only here to claim what's mine
I have more on my mind
Don't mine me
You'll never understand
You'll never get the boy I was
Or the man I am
Or the man I shall become
Harder times
Have made a harder heart
Harder to fail
I want more
Oh yea, I said more
Harder times
Have made a harder heart
One that won't allow me to fail

Hear my Soul

Listen to my words

Listen to the sound of my heart

I am afraid of love

Before we even start

Look past my past

Help open up my gates

I believe in destiny

I believe in fate

Listen to words

Follow the sounds of my heart

I'll guide you to happiness

Although I know it's far

This travelled road has been worn

The reason it's so hard is because I have been torn

Pieces of me, have no peace

I toss and turn

Wishing I could sleep

Replaying every move

I ever made

Having flashbacks of how my heart began to fade

Help me unlock this treasure

It can be all yours

I have fought battles

I need you for these wars

Hold me tight

Until it feels right

You are my comfort

You help me sleep at night

Listen to these words

Hear the whispers of my soul

If love is the key

Then please unleash my soul

If heaven is you

I have reached my goal

Just stay with me

It's the only way I feel

Whole

Hungry for Love

Feed me now

Because I need to eat

I went to bed

But didn't sleep

You were on my mind

Having thoughts of a one of a kind

Girl I dream of you being mine

Not to own you

But to honor you

For the grace of kindness

For the passion in your heart

For the bliss that you jumpstart

I am hungry for your love

And so ready to eat

I am sitting at the table

Ready for the all you can eat

Buffet of you

Come sit with me

And enjoy this meal too

Let's say a prayer

Before we indulge in this feast

Hungry for Love

Even in my sleep

I Used to Cry

You lie

I cry

I might not show it

I am better at holding it

So judge me not

Because you don't see tears

I am human and also have fears

Some of love

Some of pain

I loved once

So no, I am not ashamed

I am fearful

Still somehow relentless

To get through this storm

It all began once my heart was torn

So as I walk down this one-way street

Heading in the wrong direction

I am looking in a mirror

That doesn't have my reflection

I Used to Question my Luck

I used to question my luck

I used to despise my decisions

I used to wonder and worry

Then I found you

Something new and refreshing

Showing me a new path

A new way to laugh

The joy was endless

The feeling unreal

How could I have questioned things for so long

When meeting you felt like home

The look in your eyes

The feeling you give my heart

I no longer question things

I find the answers within my heart

All because I found you

I Want It

I want it

Cause it's right within my reach

I am in love

Cause of the company I keep

I want it for life

Cause it makes me all warm and fuzzy

My code word "Pineapples"

Cause we all think it's funny

I want it

And no you can't have

I got my group

And they will kick your ass

Open up this can of worms

And you'll see

I want it

I have it

But you may never see it

I Was Broken

I was broken

Tried to walk on two broken ankles

I needed you to believe in me

I needed you to believe in us

Yet, all you seen was a handicap person

A liability you couldn't depend on

But, your faith and will is what I needed

To wheel these wheels into a new direction

I was broken

I never asked you to fix me

I just asked for you to believe and trust me

That I was more than the eye could see

That I had wings even though you never seen me fly

I would die to ease your pain

But it seems you'll rather watch me die

Than to see me fly

I am broken

But I'll fix myself

And fly away from you

I've exposed my Flesh

So you can see the mess that I am
I've never been afraid to show who I am
Just not everyone deserves those moments
The passion and drive that defines my soul
Burying my success
So that you can see my mistakes
Hiding from nothing
I've exposed my flesh
So you can see I am a mess
Yet, every morning I am awakened
By his tender grace
Knowing he will always lead me to a better place
I've exposed my flesh
So you can see how well I do
Even when I am a mess

If

If I don't cry
Does that mean my soul doesn't weep?

If I don't dream
Does that mean I don't sleep?

If I don't say, "I love you"
Does that mean I don't love?

If my heart has no feeling
Does it mean I don't want love?

If my soul is adrift
Does it mean it's lost forever?

If I shed a tear
Does it make me less of a man?

If I can't feel your touch
Does it mean I am numb?

If I exposed my past
Does it mean our future will last?

If I write down my sins
Does it mean I am forgiven?

If this caged bird sings
Does anyone listen?

If you can't hear my cry
Does it mean I don't cry?

If I give you my heart
Does it mean I won't die?

If I change
Does it change us?

If I am willing to fight for you
Does it mean I want to fuss?

If I write you a love letter
Does it mean we can endure the stormy weather?

If Love is Real

If love is real
Why does it elude me?
If love is real
Why can't I touch it?
If love is real
Why does it hurt when it doesn't exist?
If love is real
Why does it abuse me?
If love is real
Why is it so hard to find?
If love is real
Why to some it's not a big deal?
If love is real
Why doesn't everyone have it?
If love is real
Then this is my deal
To accept it only if it promises not to steal my joy
Treat me like a toy
Or be shy
Tell me the truth
Even when it's easier to lie
If love is real
I will accept you
But that is my deal
If love is real

If my Heart Could Talk

If my heart could talk
It would speak more than words
It would sing you a song
Melodies of love
Enter your thoughts
Engulfing your soul
Music to your ears
Filling in the holes
Ones left by the pain of others
Nested there until
The right music came along
Each note something you yearned for
Something you knew
It was the clean water you needed
To wash away your blues
Now join me on stage
And let my heart serenade with these tunes
After sunset
Let's lie on the beach
And listen to our song on repeat
As we gaze into the sky
If only my heart could talk

If the Door Closes

Don't wait until I am dead to miss me

Because you make me feel as if I am not here

You have forced me into a life of fear

Trying to escape the dark days of my past

I saw light

And thought it was you at last

The search was over, and I could finally be at peace

Sleeping and dreaming

No longer that I need to weep

And feel the sorrows of what I had been through

I knew in my heart

It was you

That I would spend my lasting days

Having a reason to thank God and continue to praise

Dark clouds seem to reappear

Not by me but by your own fear

Fear me not; I only want your love

To share your heart

When I sent prayers up above

So let me in

Or out, I shall remain

If this door closes

Dead I will remain

Imaginary Love

I thought she loved me

But I was completely wrong

Seems all my life I been singing this song

Imaginary Love

You tore me apart

And I never want to go home

She broke down my walls

Built up my hopes

Made me so sick

That I choked on my feelings

Now I am stuck and no way of healing

Imaginary Love

You made me think that Love exist

I open my heart

Took that risk

Now I am stupid

And I am the dope

I have no way to cope

With Imaginary Love

Fooling me well

Taking me through hell

Imaginary Love

I tried it

Failed

Now I am hurt

Love, you can go to Hell

Imperfection

I am sorry for what I have become
But I am not sorry for what it will make me

I am not perfect, and I will never be
I will only strive for perfection

Judge me not for where I was
Judge me by where I have been and where I am going

Perfection would make me less than human
My imperfection helps me become better than human

So if you are looking for imperfection
Search within me, but while searching you will see how perfect life can be

Just focus on the faith within your heart
And within your imperfections will lie your perfections

In Your Arms

Don't ask me to quit
It's not in my blood
All these days
All that blood, sweat, and tears
The ability to overcome my fears
I know no easy roads
Because life has never been easy
I will rest in my grave
I have people watching me
So brave is all I can be
As the eyes of others follow me like shadows
I am afraid to look back
Don't want to trip over my future
Trying to go up
With hopes of never coming down
And if I fall
Let it be into your arms
Where you can protect me from all this worldly harm
Running towards a mirror
Full of shattered dreams
The grains in the hourglass
Continue to fall like my spirits
So if I fall
Let it be into your arms
Where you can protect me from all this worldly harm

Intentions

I had good intentions

Just not in your eyes

You cursed me

Thinking all my love

Was filled with lies

That's your own insecurities

And misinterpretation

I am the man

That wanted to take you to a beautiful destination

Plagued by your doubt

I can't control the times I've tried

Tired from head to toe

Nowhere to go

Because my heart is with you

I had good intentions

Just not in your eyes

It Just Came to Me

It wasn't planned; it's just not me
How was I to know she was the one for me?
Too caught in my ways
Too enclosed in these four walls
Fall in Love
Man, that is for fools
I am not saying I am too cool
Just saying my heart was too cold
Stepping away from it all
I was too busy to fall
Or even see the sweetheart
She was to me
Learning to break down walls
While using those same pieces to build bridges
So that one day I can make it back to you
I know that just like a library book
Our love is well overdue
I never saw you coming
But so glad you have arrived
Just promise me
You are here forever
Hearing that makes me smile
Cause in the blink of an eye
It just came to me

It's There

I don't want to bleed anymore

Please hold me tighter

Because it lessens the pain

The rain used to cleanse my soul

But the scars have made me cold

I want to be free

Like a bird in the sky

No matter what I do

My wings won't let me fly

I'm running out of breath

Cause I have ran so far

That I ran from myself

Not realizing I was submerged in grief

Caged up questioning my beliefs

As my days unfold

And faith starts to melt away the cold

I am sure, Love

I will once again hold

I can't rush this moment

Or let it pass me by

I am healing, don't question why

No longer dead

Like I use to be

I see Love

Do you see me?

Ready

Set

Go

I taste love

This is a fact that I know

Jumpstart

You're my heart

You are my soul

You have turned my heart warm

Once frostbitten and cold

I am learning now to be once again whole

I know we were put together

To someday be together

To endure this stormy weather

My only worry is, do you feel the same?

Outside my temperature is warm

Inside it's freezing cold

Enter my soul

Plant a seed that will jumpstart my heart

Get my blood flowing

So we get this thing going

You for me

Me for you

All I want

Is to share my life with you

Jumpstart my heart

Because for years it's been parked

Once we are in motion

There will be no stopping us

Destination set

Place unknown

Happiness Guaranteed

Just me and you alone

Staring at forever

Leaving our past alone

Killing Me

Killing Me
With a knife or any physical contact
Your words have destroyed me
Your actions have beaten me down
The sound of your voice is so unkind
Killing me and without a gun
I tried to get away, but failed to run
Killing me
When I want to live so badly
I gave you my all, even my heart
It was all that I had
Now with no heart, or the energy to breathe
I feel like I may regain life
If I could just find a way to leave
Wearing my heart on my sleeve
Until it was all wore out
Without knowing what's all this about
And no way out
Killing Me
With no physical abuse in sight

Kindle Hearts

Tears of joy

Tears of pain

Loving you has driven me insane

I thought it was just love

Then I realized I am in love

I want to give you the world

I just need you to understand

These problems are deeper than you can see

I am only me

When you are in my arms

The world is against me

I feel all I have is you

But, you have turned cold

So what do I do?

Alone again

When all I want is you

It's cold outside, but so are you

Seeking love that will never go cold

I can carry us to forever

If you could see through the pain

If we can just endure

Together we have so much to gain

Tears of joy

Because there will be

No more pain

Just two kindled hearts

With the love and happiness at our reign

Last Intimate Encounter

Passion, lust, and love
We shared all of the above
Combine these things
And we have intimacy
I know we used to share these moments
Now they are far, far away
I wanted this for a lifetime
It only lasted a blink of an eye
I cannot lie; I wanted it so bad
It makes me want to cry
The thought of our last intimate encounter
Is like no other
I want to take this intimate encounter further
One last chance
To get back to that high
I will chase it for a lifetime
That is no lie
Last intimate encounter
I want you one more time
Just to reach that high one last time
Last intimate encounter
Come one more time

Layers of Love

Tear away my layers

And my soul is green

Raw, fresh and very clean

Protected by shells

While it burned in hell

I am here

Afraid to fail

In the back of my mind

Feeling she will one day bail

On what we had

On what we were building

The layers may fall

But the wall still may appear

I wish I had an answer

Keep trying is my solution, my dear

If we work together maybe, we

Will build something higher than my walls

But if this fails, then that fall will hurt

The higher we climb

And the more we build

The more on the table

For others to steal

Given the history of this troubled soul

Tear away my layers

And my soul may still be cold

How do I know the conditions of my soul?

When I put it in an icebox

I left home

With no intentions to return

If it thaws out

It may have freezer burn

So tear away the layers

It may just blow your mind

Keep pulling away

And my heart you will find

Learning to Love Again

Learning to love again
Because I no longer know how to
Echoes of my beating heart pulsate
Like ripples on a lake
Trying to learn to love again
Is like drinking venom from a snake
Open your eyes so that you can see through my pain
Kind words and your gentle touch used to ease me to sleep
Now those same things are the reasons I can't sleep
Putting the training wheels of love back in motion
Learning to love amongst this commotion
The pain of love will not let me sleep
I know last time I was there, I got in too deep
Now the shadow of love is a creep
I won't stop until
I learn how to love
Or it puts me six feet deep
Learning to love again
Even if it's only in my sleep

Letter to Old Self

I don't know where to start
So I write this from my heart
I don't know where I went
But I am ready to go back
To being whom, I used to be
Not to backtrack
But to get me back
Somehow I used to be a man
But got lost in boyish ways
So I got go back to repping me hard
Wait until you see me again
I will be so high
And it won't be from drugs
I just miss my old self
Look at the mess I caused
I can only blame myself
Dear old self
This is a letter to you

Let me be Your Last

Leave your past with your last

Let me be your first after the worst

I know in your heart you felt cursed

Let this be a blessing for us both

Leave your past with your last

And let's build forever one second at a time

One memory after another

Until the last will no longer matter

And I'll be your first of a lifetime

You'll be my forever

Leave your past with your last

Let's make this our first

And make it last a lifetime

Let me be your first after the worst

Remove that curse

And be your blessing you never seen coming

Like No Other

There comes a moment
Like no other
Similar to the love of a mother
That you can't seem to let go
Despite the fear
The doubt
The pain
You realize
That this is true love
One of a kind
Rare
Like world peace
Moving your spirit
Touching your soul
Creating a new you
Holding you tight
Around like your shadow
Take control
Take care
This is love like no other
Similar to the love of a mother

Like the First Time

It's like I've fallen in love like the first time

I thought my past sins, would prevent me from a win

Over and over again

I took major hits to the chin

Trying to convince myself that love was deceitful

Vigorous, vicious, pressuring me to quit

Determined to prove my past would erase my

Chance at a happy future

It's like I've fallen for love

Like the first time

Reminding myself of what was wrong

Convinced I am not my past

Wishful and wise that

I am falling in love for the last time

As if it was my first time at falling in love

Listen to these Words

Forget the paper and the pen

Listen to these words

So I can tell the world

About my struggle

I was raised by a village

I have a loving mother

Doesn't mean I wasn't cold even when I had covers

Let me uncover the facts

So you can take this data

Analyze and assume

Thinking you know my pain

And you can see my wounds

No I won't be contained

What remains is what I want you to see

Try to understand the village nurtured a tree

So it could branch out and hold others up

I am just here counting my blessings

Trying to avoid the mistakes

I made while life was teaching me a lesson

Forget the pen and paper

Listen to these words

Live 4ever

I look in the sky thinking I will never die

Then I look back and realize we all will die

Sometimes I recall the past, and I want to cry

Living each day cause it could be my last

Instead of worrying about the day I go

I will just touch everyone I know

That way when I do go

There will be a piece of me

I live forever and no one will

Ever know

Lost and Lonely

I have made four right turns
With four different women
Now I am right back where I started
Lost and lonely
Trying to change the locks on the doors of my heart
I thought by making all the right turns
Things would somehow be right
But I'm left with nothing
Sitting at the intersection of
Pain and Desperation
Still healing from each one of those separations
Where can I turn when there are no more turns left?
Trying to find love
When there is no love left
Somehow love has become my death
Eager for better
I put words in this letter
So it will quiet the storm
Until I my heart can recover
From the pain of this harsh weather

Lost within Myself

Lost within myself

My feelings no longer flowing

I have been so numb; I can't even tell you where I am going

Lost within

Because I am without

Love which led to no emotions

Flipping through my past

Like it was pages from a book

Lost within

Going without

Searching for meaning

When there is no meaning to love

Cuddling myself when I need a hug

Lost within myself

Since it's the safest place I know

Lost within

I have nowhere else to go

Love Addiction

The first time I took that hit, it was like no other

I ran home and told my mother

She saw the glow in my eyes

The extra energy in my step

Saw my high, and never slept

Floating on clouds

Looking down at the stars

Man this high had taken me to Mars

I realized I was an addict

Chased that first love high

Not seeing I had become a fiend

Love addiction

Man that drug mean

It had me lost, broken, and confused

Listening to love songs saying that is just like me

I should've been in a straitjacket

With no key

Addicted to love

Like crack to base head

Love addict

Now I'm addicted

Chase the high

As if it was a sickness

My prognosis

Love addiction

Love Battle

I am fighting with me

So I can't fight with you

I have been battered and abused

My inner soul

So much that it turned my heart cold

Weak, dazzled, and hanging on by a thread

Looking into my eyes

They are bloodshot red

The beginning is dead

So there is no future in me

Fighting with you is no option

Fighting for you is a priority

Let me rest

So I can take the world off my shoulder

I can't breathe these conflicts

Heavier than boulders

So let me fight me

But don't fight me too

My soul was red

But has begun to turn blue

Open your eyes

Before opening your heart

If this is what you want

Where do we start?

Battered and bruised

Who do I accuse?

For the crime of the year

They damaged my heart

Ripped away my soul

Left me with a fire

But didn't leave the coal

So I shall burn away the dead flesh

Attempt to be my best

Settling for nothing

Unless it's the best

Open these doors

That used to shield my heart

If you enter

I shall never let you depart

Love Question

Life without Love is
No life at all
If I happen to fall?
Will you catch me?
If I stumble and trip
Will you be there to pick me up?
If my heart has been abused
And my soul restless
Will you take the pressure?
To help ease the pain
Will you soothe me?
While my energy I regain
If my past is dark
And my heart lost its spark
Will you still trust me with your heart?
If I offer you the world
But give you a state
Can we still make you happy?
Even when I make mistakes
I am asking you these love questions
Hoping Love is the answer

Love Scare

Peek-a-boo

Love, is that you?

If it goes away

I used to want you

But I would rather you not stay

Please remove yourself from my presence

You scared me lifeless

And that I will remain

I have no more energy for your games

Let this story end

And I shall allow a new one to begin

Love stare

Love scare

Me no more

I have packed my bags

And I am moving away

If you like, you are more than welcome to stay

Feast on the past

Reminisce on bliss that didn't last

Love Scare?

No thanks, I'll pass

Lovely Lies

Lovely lies
That is all I hear
Like you saying you love me
And I am your true love
But those lovely lies
Are like bittersweet scars
They will only get you so far
So keep speaking those lovely lies
And I keep smiling as if I care
Don't you dare
Speak words that have no truth
Your lovely lies
Are like decay that started at the roots
So keep away from me
You dirty little parasite
I won't fight for the truth anymore
I will just take your lovely little lies
Store them away
Package them up
And send you and those lovely lies
Far, far, away

Lying to Myself

Forgive me father

For I know of my sins

I tried to win

And ended up losing in the end

I put my heart, before my faith

Which lead to me lying to my soul

That questioned my faith as a whole

Father, I know better

Still, I can't explain my actions

Good intentions with bad results

Or a man on a mission with no regards to the consequences

Father, I have been lying to myself

Telling myself that I know what love is

If love was looking me right in the face

I wouldn't know it from a hole in a wall

Which would be no different than the hole in my heart

Lying to myself

To try to heal this hole that exists

But my outlook on love is foggy with an overcast of mist

Maybe I will know love again

When she gives me that one of a kind kiss

Until then lying to myself

Gives me the smallest risk

Tale of the Sexes

All men are dogs

All women minds jump around like frogs

There are not good women

Nice guys finish last

The last guy I dated

Only wanted a piece of ass

She only after my money

Man both sexes be acting funny

Why he got to lie

Why she trifling

Girl, I can't like him, cause he ain't hood

Man she slept with my boy, I know she ain't no good

Tale of the Sexes

Who is right, who is wrong?

Unless we keep it real

We will always end up alone

That is the tale of the sexes

Meowing Soul

I gave you the world

But why am I curled up

In a ball

Crying my eyes out

Feeling like I just took the plunge of death

Forced into silence

Cause my heart can't speak the words

Bending so far

That I want to break

But I refuse

Cause I will not fall apart

Bent out of shape

But refusing to break

You beat my heart so bad

That it is in prime shape

Bending, but never broken

Are the walls of my heart

I am curled in this ball

These tears cut my face

Cause the pain in them is so sharp

They expose my human nature

As my animal instinct prowls

I will roar

But my soul meows

Midnight Train

Looked into your eyes

I could tell that the purity was gone

I was no longer drunk from your love

It was more like a sickness of your touch

Your eyes tell me a story

That your mouth won't reveal

You softened my heart

Then you went in for the kill

Going insane by the tone of your eyes

Inside my soul is hurting, seeking reasons not to cry

At one point I could rest in soul for life

Now I am packing my bags, headed on the next midnight train

I said long ago I was done playing those games

So your eyes told me the story

I will just walk away with and save myself the shame

I am running this time

If you decide to look for me

I am on the midnight train

My exit is "No Games"

My destination is "Love without Shame"

All aboard

This midnight train

Misty Oceans

Dark days

Stormy nights

I miss having someone next to me

To help me with this fight

To brighten up my days

The days as dark as night

To protect me during stormy nights

When the rain and wind have beaten me to a pulp

I wish I had your love

And your tender touch

As I roam alone for no particular place or time

I sit in the sand writing these rhymes

They keep me sane

Cause lord knows

I am losing my mind

Touched by a pain

That has yet to heal

If I knew where I could find love

I would steal it away

Spend the rest of my life with it

We could run away

Though that kind of love is only a dream

Dark days

Stormy nights

I am used to it

That is my nightmare

As well as my dream

Misunderstood

Look me in the eyes
Tell me the person you see
Do you look at me how you want me to be?
Or looking at me for what I want to be?
Destined for Greatness is what my heart yearns
But the friends around me would rather watch me burn
Caught up in a life that leads to broken hearts
My intentions are good
They just don't get me very far
Misunderstood soul
Who heart has become cold
From all the abuse
The countless excuses
Stuck in a world of millions
Feeling like the only one here
I am afraid to awake
Because of my fears
The tears I shed
Are not of joy
But a way to escape
Because being misunderstood
Carries too much weight
So I shed these tears
Accepting it as fate
Calling on God
Asking him
Never to be late
Because I am unsure
How much I can take

Monsters

God gave me the strength to forgive

And the wisdom to never forget

This monster that lurks

In the dark

Was caused by you

I loved you

And my heart remained true

After countless months of pain

My soul and faith still remain

I will not let this monster you created

Get the best of me

In the end, the only call you will answer

Is from my God, you see?

This monster still lurks

In the pit of my soul

Latched on trying to turn me cold

Monsters from the past

Are now closer than ever

I put my faith in God

To handle this endeavor

Monsters are demons

Seeking to destroy my soul

Through my faith in God

My soul will remain whole

As these monsters

Try and turn my heart cold

More than Life

I am so alive

I love you more than life itself

I put you first

Because you are the sparkle in my eye

You are the fire in my heart

My day starts with you

My last thought before I sleep is of you

You don't have to cry, but if you do, I'll dry your eyes

I've exposed more than just my soul

I've exposed everything, because without you

I am no longer whole

You've filled every hole

Closed every gap

My heart is trapped

With no desire to be released from your grasp

I am alive

Forever me and you

This thing will last

I love you more than life itself

My Favorite Song

Her smile has a glow

Little did I know she would disappear for years

But fate reconnected us

So we talk about our joys and fears

Listening to her every word

As if it was music from my favorite song

Lyrics dancing around like clouds in the sky

How high can we go

When the beats of our conversation just flow

Who knows what will be

I just look at her smile

And joy and happiness is all I see

Her smile has a glow

One that I'll never forget

One I am glad to know

My First Glance

I knew she was the one

From my first glance

I just needed a chance

To show her

I finally felt her touch

And told her I was in love

She said she loved me

From the look in her eyes

I was destined for disappointment

I knew I could never have her

The way I wanted her

She would never see the true man I am

I knew she was the one

From first glance

I just knew in my heart she would never

Give me a fair chance

I was destined for disappointment

My Only Thoughts

You are a part of me
And no matter what
You will be in my every thought
Every fiber of my soul
Is a story that is told by you
Even when my heart is blue
It's the memories we shared
That keeps it straight
You are a part of me
And no matter what
You will be in my every thought

Naked and Afraid

Here I am
Naked and afraid
I have faith
But my heart is numb
How come I feel this way?
What part of my past
Caused these consequences
Here I am
Naked and afraid
Ready for love
But Lord knows I am afraid
I know my past wants to haunt me
I see it every time I close my eyes
Lies from her lies from me
Lured us into lust
Now we are two broken souls
Holding on to the past
Here I am
Cleansed of my sins
If you try again I think we can put our past
In the wind
And win again
Here I am
Naked and afraid

Nine Plus Years

Nine plus years of running from my fears

Keeping my life in privacy, to hide my pain

I know what pain looks like, I looked it right in the face

I would rather expose the truth than to live a lie

I have fought so hard to get back all that I lost

Nine plus years of running from my fears

Finally giving someone the key

Thinking they would use it

Instead they leave me a note at the door

Saying "Thank you, but no thanks"

So I finally decided to start over

And get back everything I lost

Only to realize I lost more in finding myself

Than I lost in the nine-plus years of running from my fears

How do you rebuild something with missing pieces?

The key is the key

Unlocking the treasure and using what's in the chest

To make the best of what you have

I refuse to not get this on the page

Because I have to find a way to tell you

Nine plus years of running from my fears

Now all I want to do is live my years

With you

I got your note

The key is still at the door

Waiting for you to come back

And open the door

And let's put this puzzle together

Nine plus years of running from my fears

All I want to do is make this imperfect picture

As perfect as possible exposing all the scars, the flaws

Because together we can defy the laws of Love

No Acting

One second they are here

Another they are gone

Trials and tribulations

Ups and downs

Broken glass

Broken hearts

When we clash

Will we overcome?

Allow it to last

We are the cast

But let's act

Let's play our roles

Emerge ourselves

Completing one another

So that we will remain whole

Holding on to the good

Erasing the bad

Touching each other's heart

So that this love will last

Open your heart

I'll give you my soul

Give me your hand

That is the only way we can remain whole

Nothing Remains

Faith seeps through my hands
Like water down a drain
Trying to be strong
But some people around me
Driving me insane
Built on being real
Manage to construct a heart of steel
Left a small hole in it
That I am afraid will get me killed
Letting too many in
And not enough out
At the rate I am going
I am down for the count
Should I shed these soft layers?
And let my shell reappear
My only fear
Is I will miss my true love, my dear
Stuck in my misery
As trouble eats at my flesh
Can you come to my rescue?
I am in need of rest
If you are too busy
I understand
I will just sit here
As my heart
Leaks out my chest
Until just like my soul
There is nothing left

Numb

My soul so damaged
I can feel no more
Sitting in the rain
But the storm scares me no more
So numb
From the abuse over the years
It's raining, and those are just my tears
Holding on to this simple thread
Sometimes I think a bullet to my head
Would feel much better
I am sure I wouldn't even feel that pain
Running towards love
And yet I have nothing to gain
Numb from head to toe
Standing on the front line
They are usually the first to go
Let me wonder away
Weltered as I may
I am numb
And numb I will stay
Until death takes the numb away

On my Sleeve

Here is my heart

I used to wear it on my sleeve

I decided to give it to you

I feel you will never leave

Opening up my heart

Like I never did before

Instead of giving you pieces of me

I'll just give you my whole heart

You can see the scars

See the paths of my past

I am giving you my heart

I want you to be my last

I will admit it was not easy

But your love erased the pain of my past

Here is my heart

I used to wear it on my sleeve

If you ever leave

My heart will forever be with you

Because you gave me the strength

To give you my heart

Instead of wearing it on my sleeve

Once Again

I once had a dream
And the dream included you
I had the glass slipper
But somehow lost you
I'm determined to find you once again
I put away my pain
So I can regain strength
To love
Not only myself
But you once again
When I thought I needed space
I was wrong
Now that I have to face
Traveling along this road
That we once shared together
I blocked you
Like rain on leather
Whether you come back to me
Or Not
I won't stop on my journey
I may have gotten lost along the way
But with every dark night, there is a brighter day
So as I voyage down these dark roads
My only hope is to find you along the way
If I get lost, I just hope I collect wisdom along the way
That will help me put the pieces of this puzzle together
As I dream about you
Once Again

Open Gates

You may not believe in me

Or even know my heart

I'll pour it out to you

If you just give me the chance

I know I have made mistakes in the past

Which has caused the walls of my present

The future could be bright

If we do this thing right

Let's trade hearts

Nurture them as if they're our own

Expose them to the world

But always keep them safe at home

Trust in me

As I trust in you

I want love

Only from you

Embrace these thoughts

Follow these lines

And we can be together

Until the end of time

Open my Heart

I'll open my heart

To let you in

If you promise to be with me til the end

I have been hurt in the past

But I got to find a way to last

The wombs are free

And I will not settle for less

I will give you my heart

And all my best

But allow me to trust you

Permit me to learn you

Let me love you

Open your heart

So I can

Open my heart

2

U

Open Your Eyes, Before You Open Your Heart

Trust Everyone

Like you trust no one

Relate to the relatable

Control the controllable

Never let anyone control you

Open your eyes

Before you open your heart

If you didn't know, it was fire

But you didn't get burnt

Search for the lesson

And the blessing will follow

Give your joy away

Never let it be taken away

Treat each morning

Like a new beginning

Convincing yourself

That each day you wake up

You still have a chance at winning

Remember bad things

Happen to good people

But plant those seeds

Watch as they blossom

If you planted bad ones

You're as dead as a possum

Life gives us many chances

We just never know when our last one will be

So open your eyes

Before you open your heart

Ask for forgiveness

Learn the lesson

And remember, always to count your blessings

Opening Up

Opening up is the hardest thing to do

Maybe it's simple for you

You need to know what I been through

Endless heartbreaks

Countless broken promises

Dreams shattered right before my eyes

Being told the truth, when they were just delicate lies

So when you give me these guidelines of what I should be

Maybe letting me be me, is the ultimate key

I'll unlock your heart and fulfill our dreams

Just believe in this cause

I know times will be rough and even very dark

When those times come, we have to be each other's spark

Come and let us be each other's support system

Not because we need each other

Just because we are perfect for each other

Seeing our flaws, yet still painting the perfect picture

With every stroke of success, we will see our errors

But never having a failure

If we can be strong and always be together

So opening up is the hardest thing to do

Give me some time

In the end

All I want is you

Out of Breath

I have been fighting for you

I have been running from it

I have been building on it

I have been beaten up by it

I have held it

I have lost it

I have wounds from it

I miss it

I want it

I want it forever

I want to know it again

I want to share it

I want to know the meaning of it

I am out of breath

Reenergize me

Love

Outside the Lines

Don't color outside the lines

Live in this box because it's safe

These are your rules

But I felt those lines weren't for me

I wasn't the same

I grew up being ashamed

But then I realized at an early age

That if I didn't act now

It would be too late

So before I bleed out

I had to speak out

Become my own man, not what someone told me what to be

How could I forget

I was in a hurry to get to a place unknown

So I had to practice

To strive for perfect

And even though I color outside the lines

Doesn't mean my picture isn't as beautiful as yours

These are your rules

Let me play by mine

Part Time Lover

I can't fall easily
But I sure fall hard
I'll give you my all
Once you make that call
If my heart answers
Then you are the one
Open arms with a pure heart
My soul is dead
But you will be the jumpstart
Part-time lover
Part-time friend
I refuse to be either
It's like living in sin
Give me your all
And we both will win
If I had to judge me with you
It will be a perfect 10

Particle of My Past

Pieces of my past
Still linger in my system
Attacking me like a common cold
Penetrating my present
So I can never have a future
These particles hanging around my heart
Like shrapnel from a bomb
My heart ready to explode
I can't remain calm
Particles of my past
Will you please pass away?
The longer I keep you
The shorter I stay
Particles of the past
Please fade away
One of us has to go
And love is my reason to stay
Particles of my past
Please fade away

Passion

Passion is what passion does
I want to find love
Not the fake or the fickle
But the kind that is stronger than nickel
I know it exists
Because I saw it once before
Somehow I managed to close that door
Give and be given to
I want to love unconditional
With no clause
Just to take your breath away in awe
Here I am
Here I stand
Ready to be yours
I am standing here
Willing to reopen those doors
Passion is what passion does
So Ms. Passionate
Make me yours

Perfect Picture

If you are looking for the perfect picture

I am wasting your time

If you're seeking to be perfect with me

Then all I have is time

I have the purest heart

The strongest mind

I will be the river

That flows to the sea

If you meet me there

That is all we will need

If you're looking for the perfect picture

That is me

If you're looking for someone to move mountains

Then you can find that in me

If you're searching for comfort

I am not hard to find

If you are looking to find endless love

Stand with me

While we take this picture

Then and only then will it be perfect

Picture perfect will never be a

Perfect picture

Pen to Paper 2

The only thing I can trust is my pen

It keeps me up but it knows my sins

It has never turned its back on me

It opened my heart to an endless canvas

So I could free these thoughts

Never judging or making me question its loyalty

Dear paper, forgive me for the pain of this pen

It said you needed us as bad we needed you

I couldn't be me without either of you

So let's remain true to one another

We seem to be three lost souls

Having something that the other needs

So put your trust in me and I'll never disappoint

You are more than a muse, you amuse me

You inspire me, you help me grow

You know even when I don't know

So this is my devotion and dedication to you

I'll never leave your side

Pen to paper 2

We have our roles

We know what to do

Phantom Friends

They say what you see is what you get

But if I see a sheep, doesn't mean I won't get a wolf

So tear away the wool, expose the skin

Cause everyone that is around you

May not be your friend

So what you see is far beyond what you imagine

Picture life as if you are a caged animal

Ready to attack

Because if you don't, someone will hunt you

Ready to kill your image

Destroy your soul

Abandon you, leaving you out in the cold

So pull away skin

Cause just as the shell of a coconut may seem rough

The joy of the middle is worth the fuss

So beware of the sheep, because some of them bite

Because not all those around you

Will do things right

So open your eyes

Before exposing your heart

Cause the second you turn away

It could be pierced with a dart

"Thought you cared for me?"

I did

But I was just waiting for you to open up your lid

So I could enter

And destroy your fruits

It wouldn't work

Unless you allowed me

To find your roots

So accept this poison

May you rest in peace

This was not forever

It was a terminating lease

On your heart, your dreams, your goals

I wouldn't be happy

Until I turned your every fiber into coal

Accept your demise

You trusted me

But never notice the venom in my eyes

From hello

Phantom friends

Plant their seeds of lies

Pieces of Me

They say it's better to have loved and lost

Than never to have loved at all

Well, what if you loved so much until you lost it all?

How do you regain it?

How do you put a puzzle back together?

When you can't even find all the pieces

So don't tell me who to love or how to love

This I know

Just because I have a different way

In the way, I show

Doesn't make me less of a lover

I just have covered my skin with a

Protected coat

Shipped my heart off in a boat

And bled my soul in the river

Left it to float

So all you have is a superhuman being

With no superpowers

Just a super sense of intuition

Mind, body, and soul on a mission

To protect itself

Until I can relocate all my pieces

Please Forgive Me

Lord please forgive me

I am aware of my sins

If I could do it all over again

I would be better

I am bothered by my past

The skeletons keep coming alive

I feel more dead than I do alive

I just want to love and live

Lord please forgive me

I know I've sinned

How can I win the heart of my true love

If my past keeps creeping up on me

It's like my shadow

Am I destined to live in darkness

Because of my transgressions

Please set me free

Don't set me up for failure

I am ready to love and be loved

Send me your blessing from above

Lord please forgive my sins

I've found my love

This time I want to win

Poetic Insanity

Call me crazy

Call me insane

But step one, step into my brain

And you will need an ordained priest

To release you from the trauma

The passion, the rage, the love, the pain

Molding me into this being, a creature

A shell of what I used to be

So poetry has become my invisible friend

Guiding my insanity

Making it my friend

Poetically crazy to some it may seem

But what is a river without a stream

It's like being asleep

And all you missing is the dream

So I hold my tongue

And let my words do the talking

Either be real to me

Or I am walking

Cause I can accept insanity

But I can't take your lies

I'll be the bug spray

You can remain the flies

Poetically Insane

So crazy, I no longer cry

Public Service Announcement

I will fight for you, but not with you

I will respect you as much as you respect me

I will ride for you, but won't die over you

I will give you my last if it means we stay together

I will stand in the cold, and endure the harshest weathers

I will live for you, as long as you live for me

I will love you first, but I will always fall in love last

I have a troubled past, but I will not let it affect our future

I have scars that are deep, but with you, in my arms, I will be at peace

I will be all I can for you, as long as we can live as one but love as two

I will walk through the door if you just leave it open

I don't have much, but I will give you my all

I just need to know that you will catch me if I ever fall

In love with you

Purity

My heart is pure as gold

My intentions seem to turn into coal

I wish I could take a snapshot of my soul

So you could see its purity

Painted as if I am a black sheep

So inside my heart weeps

Asking for someone to see the good in my actions

But positive outcomes is something I am lacking

Open your eyes and allow them to focus

Sometimes I wish I could perform magic

Like Hocus Pocus

Give me a wish

Grant me serenity

So I can finally find peace

Tired of tossing and turning

My heart and soul are burning

Flames of pain

Because of the coal they throw

I got one life to live

So I must go

Move on

Move out

Leaving what I can't control

In God's hand

All I can do

Is be the best man I can

When my time comes

And my fears are exposed

Just keep one thing in mind

I mean well

I might not always get it right

But my heart is pure

Pursuit of Love

Eluded by Love

The pursuit of happiness

Will never be that close again

The chase, the challenge resulted

In pain that I still carry years later

The pursuit of Love

Led me down a road of glory

That ran me off a cliff

Into a sea of darkness

Which sucked me into a cave

Where I hid my heart, my soul, and my voice

So that no one could ever hear my cries

Where I could just fade away and die

The pursuit of Love

Has eluded me for such a long time

That I am prepared for a lifetime without Love

That is why I am no longer in the pursuit of Love

So I may never know what happiness is again

Puzzle Pieces

Broken into pieces years ago

All I have is impartial objects to show

Showing you where I have been

The blessings, the sins

By no means perfect

Striving to be perfected

For many years letting my heart go neglected

Puzzle pieces are all that is left

Turn my heart off

Now it's stuck on tone deaf

Bittersweet memory

Paint a vivid picture

That shows my imperfections

Piecing me back together

Nearly impossible in this stormy weather

Still caring

Despite all the hurt

What happens to my previous work?

Stronger as mule

Tank on full

Why are my thoughts stubborn like a bull?

Did all the right things

Received all the wrong results

These broken pieces

Seem entirely my fault

Am I truly the blame?

Or just ashamed?

That I was never the person

I thought I was

This puzzle piece

All I have

To solve this mystery of mine

I guess I will rebuild myself

One puzzle piece

At a time

Until this puzzle piece

Produces a picture

Of what I was, what I am, and what I shall be

Puzzle pieces, piece me back together

So I can reveal myself to the world

Open wounds, scars, tears, and pain

When I put it all together

You will have a story of a man

Whose heart has endured a year of stormy weather

Red to Blue

Starting to think it's true

As I watch my heart fade from red back to blue

I start to realize I care way too much

About you

The things you do

And that is the reason my heart is back to blue

What do I do?

I know I love you

But the pain is unbearable

Yet, I am afraid to leave

Cause deep in my heart, I truly believe

That you are the one strictly for me

Or maybe I am too blind

Or just don't want to see

That your love for me

Just doesn't exist

Or maybe I am not important enough

To be on your top list

I wish I didn't love you so much

That really makes me pissed

As my heart fades back to blue

One day I hope our love

Will somehow become true

Reflections of the Past

Reflection of the past
Molds my present
This hinders my future
I will cherish you
If you can embrace
Within these walls
I am fighting to break them down
The sound of your voice
Soothes the pain
I am hurt
Yet, you are not the blame
Ashamed to truly expose my soul
Giving you the chance
Well that is me being bold
Reflection from the mirror
Frighten me daily
As I reminisce on how I got to this stage
Closed up
Frightened, yet still enraged
Gentle giant to some
With a stone heart in a cage
If you find a way to love me
That is the key to the cage
Your tears of pain and those of joy
Will transform my stone heart
From rocks and rubble
To a beating soul protected in your bubble

Because I will be able to share it once again

Releasing the pain

And clear up the rain

Giving it to you

And yours it will remain

Reflections of the past

Are only reflections of what was

The present is here

My future is your love

Repeat Offender

When I said, "I'd be gone"
I didn't think you would let others enter our home
I tried to talk
But you would speak
I spent many nights losing sleep
Now as I stare into the mirror
Afraid of my own reflection
Reflect on what is left
When all my rights turned into wrong
It seems all I can sing is these sad songs
In a four-corner room
Scream at the top of my lungs
Saying I won't make the same mistakes again
But as my present turns into my past
My future blows in the wind
Running out of room to breathe
Trying to find a way to leave
Stuck in misery, dancing with my grief
When I said was leaving
I didn't mean leaving you
I needed a break
To realize it was you
I won't allow the same mistakes again
Seem you won't give me the same opportunities again
So I will continue to stare at my reflection
Reflecting on how much I am afraid of what I see in the mirror

Rubber Bands

The closer you get; the further I push you away

You can't see what I need

You can't know what I have seen

I say it can't be so

I think of all the times my heart has been scarred

Even though you mean the world to me

I keep stretching us like rubber bands

Knowing that if I keep the tension between us

Someday it will pop

I love you

But my heart says stop

I want to go on

But the rubber bands are all I can hold on to

I look at you and see that you are true

I just don't want to be scarred

So the closer you get, the further I stretch our love

I keep pulling; hoping it will pop

If I sabotage our love

Maybe you will stop giving me something

That I apparently can't handle

I'll keep pulling on this rubber band

Cause when I let go

The recoil from the tension

Will surely dismantle

My love that I stretched too far

Just like rubber bands

Ruin Me

Ruin me

Like only you can

I wanted to be your stand up man

But you kept putting me down

Ruin me

It is all you want to do

I carried our weight

You just didn't see us through

Ruin me

Cause you rather see me rot

My heart is dead

The love disease I caught

Ruin me

Cause you ran me into the ground

Lost all that I loved

Left it all behind

Ruin me

Like only, you know how

Our relationship summed up

A long Green Mile

Ruin me, ruin me

Are the words that echo from our past

I did you a favor and packed your bags

Set them outside the door

You ruined me

You filthy little whore

I realized I don't love you anymore

Drop the keys

As you leave out my door

You will not ruin me

Anymore

Safe with You

Don't ask me why
I really don't know
I want you to enter
But just scared you know?
Not trying to sell you a dream
Just want to be happy
Where that leads me
Versus where I am going
I still have scars
Yet, I am still going
Trapped by my past
And it's not your fault by any means
I just saw life with you
And seen happiness it seemed
Scarred to death
Ready to exit stage left
I took one more deep breath
And emerge me into you
Now I am stuck
Cause I have fallen for you
So don't let me go
I have found a new home
So stay with me
So we can turn this into our own

Scar Tissue Love

I was drifting away
Then the love in your voice
Put me back afloat
Now I'm gathering myself
Trying to recoup
From the scars
That never healed
Together with you
Now that is something real
I must admit
The thought of togetherness
Scares me pale
If you'd seen my wounds
You would think I had a fight with hell
I never saw a star so bright
Until I looked into your eyes
I must confess
The soul of love I no longer possess
I do ask of you to plant a seed
Water it well
And in the end
At the alter
We will have a story to tell
You are heaven
And you have pulled me from the depths of hell

Secrets

Behind closed doors

It's only me, you, and these four walls

I want you

You want me

He has you

She has me

But I'll play my role

But my heart wants more

These secrets poison my heart

The love we share can only be the antivenom for so long

I know they talk

I hear the whispers in the air

But I don't want to share you anymore

Let's eliminate the guilty

And put this little secret behind

I want you to be mine

They will have to understand

I am your man

You my girl

I am ready to offer you the world

But we must leave our luggage

Go on our new journey

We are each other's a secret

Either be with me

Or it is me that must go

The poison of these secrets

Have eroded my soul

So let him go

So I can have all of your soul

She is a distant memory

I no longer love

Come with me

Let's bond our love

You say you can't leave

And you can't tell him the truth

So I am your little secret

That will die within you

Secret Intentions

The love I had for you was no secret

Yet, I protected every secret you gave me

Holding on to intentions that meant well

Yet, somehow always putting you thru hell

I know you had to bail

You had every reason

I know what we had was meant for more than a few seasons

As I recall and reflect

On what to do next

I hope my next investment will yield

Unlimited returns

Or maybe you'll return to me

The love I had for you was no secret

I just kept us a secret for far too long

That's where it all went wrong

Seeping In, Weeping Out

The more I let you in

The further you moved out

Leading me down a road

But you decided to take a detour

Which led to hurting me at the core

I wanted more of you

You wanted less of us

I would give you the world

Actually, it is a must

I wasn't here for lust

I came for love

Left broken

I gave you my soul

My most prized token

I am learning to let it burn

But it is burning me back

If I had one wish

I would have you back

Let me count the stars

That was my view of you

You tore me apart

And I still can't be through with you

Shattered

Once a mirror is broken
It is never the same.
The image will always be distorted.
Cuts obtained from picking up the shards
Are painful reminders of its sharp edges,
But the joy isn't in the broken mirror.
The joy is looking past the cracks,
Past the edges, past the pain, to see the beauty.
True beauty is a reflection of what you see,
Not what others tell you
You're supposed to see.
Look deeper. Look beyond the fragments.
The mirror may be broken,
But the beauty remains.

She Had a Handful of Maybes

She had a handful of maybes

And all it caused was doubt

I doubt we will never have what we had

I don't want it anyways; I want more

I want better

So, if all you have is a handful of maybes

Then maybe this won't work

Give me lifetime of loyalty and dedication

She had a handful of maybes

In my eyes

In the end, she has nothing

Because maybe she loved me or maybe she doesn't

I'll leave her alone with her

Handful of maybes

She Had No Idea of Her Value

She had no idea her value

She was priceless

She was the reason I woke up

She was the reason I wouldn't stop going

She was all I needed

In a world full of wants

I only wanted to give her the feelings she gave me

She couldn't see how majestic she was

She was priceless

I just wish she knew her worth

Because she was worth everything to me

Yet, she saw very little value in herself

She was the reason I smiled

She's Tired

Ready to rise
I see the pain in her eyes
She is tired of trying
She tired of crying
She tired of all the hurt
Afraid of any one man trying to touch her heart
She needs convincing
Knowing if I tell her I love her
She will run faster and further away
Trying to create a union
But she's so close to the edge
So I keep my distance
Not prepared to fail
I see the pain in her eyes
Cause she don't cry much
She's afraid to show her heart
Cause she is afraid of exposing her scars
Ready to rise
And heal all the pain I see in her eyes

Shower in the Shower

As the water flows from the shower

So do the tears from my eyes

The best place to hide em

So no one can see my pain

Let them flow, as they head to the drain

Washing away the dirt of my past

Trying to freshen up for my present

As I get ready for the future

Contemplating where to store these tears

As I lie in this shower trying to wash away these fears

Shower in the shower

It all feels like rain

Each tear I shed is equal to an ounce of pain

Hoping I can regain part of the man

I used to be, but all these tears

Makes it hard to see

I hide in the shower

It seems the safest place to be

Shower in the shower

Where else can I go?

As the water flows

So does the pain

That I seem never to let go

Shower in the shower

It is where I let my past go

Side by Side

Waking up to you

Is all I want to do

We are miles apart

But our hearts and soul are side by side

I can feel you every moment of the day

Because you're in my every thought

Waking up to you

Right now is only a dream

Distance may keep us apart

But it brings us closer together

One day I won't have to imagine waking up next to you

Because one day my dream will come true

Until then, let our hearts and soul be side by side

Until that day when we can wake up side by side

Silence of Death

You asked me to trust you with my heart

You must be a damn fool

I opened up before, and you mutilated my heart

I can't be your fool again

My heart can't bare the pain

It absorbed so much turmoil

It had no room to gain

Or to grow

If you put it near you

The pain and poison

Would rot away your soul

This cold heart pain

Was the product of your touch

So if you asking me to trust you

You got life fucked up

I hold no grudge

Nor do I harness the pain

Just some scar tissue

That will always remain

Human perception

Paints a picture of life

But don't tell me about a book

If you don't read the words they write

So trust yourself and the man above

Open your heart and lead with love

Just don't be any fool

For the pain of your past

Hit delete

And protect your ass

So my heart is dramatized

But it won't repeat being a fool

I'll be your friend

Cause I can't be your lover

And I won't be your fool

Heart to Soul

I refuse to suffer once again

In your cold-hearted grip

You ripped me off once

This time, I refuse to slip

You homicide killer

I might be alive

But you are one cold-hearted killer

Six Degrees of Separation

So far from who I used to be

That not even my friends know who I am

Separated from my mind, body, and soul

The presence of certain people has turned all three cold

When shall I return? The world may never know

Lost in stars, because there is no other place to go

Separation anxiety is just a breath away

Wanting to be more than who I am now, one day

Take me back to where I used to be

So I can reflect and see where I went wrong

So I can change this station, and stop singing this sad song

Open my eyes, chase away my fears

I have been separated from myself for so long

I am not sure who I am I fear

Six degrees away

I am separated in six different ways

Someone Woke up My Soul

Someone woke up my soul

They knew somehow it was cold

I didn't show signs of frostbite

But she knew I was at the edge of defeat

She brought me to my feet

Looked me in my eyes

Said I am here

So, we will begin this battle as one

You no longer have to be in the trenches alone

We will win this war

And make it home

Our hearts are now connected

And we no longer have to worry

Let's go into battle as one

We have awaken each other souls

I seen your frostbite

You've seen my shattered soul

Love is the thing that will keep us whole

Something Borrowed

Something borrowed
Because it was never mine
I wanted love and thought I could take it from someone else
Now all I did was create a mess
If I give you my heart, just return it as it was given
No need to add abuse or any more scars
Just keep it safe and the world is ours
Something borrowed
Cause my own heart, is no longer mine
I gave it away, and somehow I can't get it back
Something borrowed
Could be fine
Why did I loan out my heart
Without having an agreement signed
Seems like I lost it in a bet
It was my fault for taking the gamble
Now my heart, my mind, and my soul are stuck in a shamble
Something borrowed
With no return address
Now I am heartless
With no way of cleaning up my mess
Next time something is borrowed
I will ensure to provide a return address
Something borrowed
Has left an empty burning feeling in my chest

Something Went Wrong

We lie in bed together

And I noticed a change in the weather

When I hold you tight

Something in my heart not right

I ask what is wrong with you

Nothing is your reply as your attitude is blue

Something went wrong

This I am sure

We at Battle

Better yet War

Either Love has lost its spark

Or you are ready to jump cart

Something went wrong

I don't know where to start

So as I watch you gaze into space

As I lose this race

Can you please help this case?

Have I been replaced?

Something went wrong

I can see it in your face

Speaking Honestly

When you looked me in my eyes
I could see the lies
I stood around
Knowing of the lies
Wanting to condemn you to hell
I could only imagine
The things I didn't know
I could only wonder why
I wanted to say goodbye
But my heart wanted to accept your lies
I would have rather been half-dead with you
It was the only reason I accepted the lies
Until the lies poisoned my insides
Rotted away my soul
Turned my heart into stone
Made all my emotions cold
Speaking honestly
When I look into your eyes
My soul cries
For holding on to those lies
Speaking honestly
All my feelings died
When all I could recall
Is how much I cried
For looking into your eyes
And seeing all those lies

Speechless Words

If I had the words
I would give them to you every second of the day
I love you
I express it in a different way
I may not say much
But I hope my love is heard well
I want to touch your soul
Like Heaven, not Hell
I want your well to overflow
With the love I want to give
I want to live in your heart
And rest in your soul
I want to be there when your days are cold
Sometimes I can't speak
But it doesn't mean I don't talk
I will carry you on days you can't walk
Just see past my words
And just follow my heart
We both have troubled pasts
That doesn't mean we can't hit
Restart
As I look into your eyes
And swim in your soul
Your presence
Has begun to fill in those holes
So these speechless words
Are all I have
They cleanse my soul
Because it's all I have

Starting Over

Starting over

Because there is nothing of you left;

Giving 100% until your existence is no longer here

How do you rebuild when there is nothing there?

How do plant a seed

Where it has no place to nurture?

When you start over, is it really you?

When you been true to others

Yet, they haven't been true to you

How can you hit restart?

Without worry about seeing the play

How can you see light, when all you seen is darkness during the day?

Starting over

When there is nothing of you left

How can I heal?

When the wounds are still there

How can I run?

When I have nowhere to go

How do I uplift myself?

When I am so low

How do I restart?

When I can't even go

Starting over is not as easy as it sounds;

I can't move on, when my feet are bound

By the cement of the past

Being stuck, abused, too many people stabbing my ass

I think I sprung a leak

And my heart and soul

Slowly seeped away

Until I fell to my knees

Gasping for air

No one was there

I don't think they care

Starting over

Restarting my past

Learning to let others kiss my ass

Starting over is no easy task

But if I am going to better

Endure the trials and tribulations of this world

I must find a new way to be strong

Standing up

Starting over

This is all I can do

Sitting in my corner

Hoping for hope

Won't get me anywhere

So if you call

And I just don't answer

It is not you it is not me

I started over

And people like you I just don't see

Starting over

Stones at the Window

She threw a stone with all her might;

I was looking out the window

When it hit, I lost sight

She didn't break it,

But it was shattered;

Still held together to protect me against the weather

From that day on looking out the window would never be the same

I kept thinking it was still perfect, which drove me insane

Thrown stones at my window

Just became a pile

Which protect me for awhile

Each new stone shattering it more

Still together, enduring more

Yet each stone hurting a little more

Stones at my window

Have become my new front door

Stop Crying, I am Still Here

I know you are thinking that I am gone,

But try not fear;

I just checked into a better place

To look over you and watch you

Keep faith, I completed my work here

And now God has called me

To look over you

I know it's natural to cry and worry

But fear no more

My pain is gone

I suffer no more

I have received my wings

And now when the clouds seem a little dark

Just begin to pray

And I will guide you through the storm

Days are brighter for me now

So I will be right above you

Until you can join me

Praise my new beginning

And understand that this is not an ending

Just my REBIRTH as an Angel of God

Sent to assist you when you can go no further

I will use my wings to cover you

This is not my last breath

It's just God's way of giving me a fresh breath of air

Again Fear not anymore I am just not by your side

I am just above you to cover you

So stop crying, I am still here.

Story of Love

Some would think I hate Love

I just don't trust Love

Love has too many elements

Too many clauses,

Too many risks,

Too many fears,

The story of Love

Is that you never can tell when it starts

When it truly ends

Or if it's really there

Love has too many forms

Too many conditions

Love is fearless,

Yet tricky

And sweet

It can make you happy

Or make you cry until you weak

Why trust something you really don't know?

Can you truly trust love?

When she is so cunning

I saw her

Decided to keep running

Story of Love

It really isn't funny

Sunken

Left with hollow holes

That were once filled

With your love

Trying to plug them

So my ship will stop sinking

Sunken by my own misery

Constantly pointing the finger at myself

Trying to tell myself there isn't anything left

I won't succumb to those doubts

Even though the days look dark

My heart knows something my head doesn't

So the struggle is real

My faith stronger than steel

That one day I'll steal your heart

Back once again

I feel like it could end in a loss

But my heart sees my effort as a win

Left with holes

That somehow I will learn to fill

As I try to feel the way I once felt

Take Me Away

Take me away

Because I don't wanna be here

Take me away

Because I want to be near you

Take me away

Because I want to breathe again

Take me away

Because there is a better place for me and you

Take me away

Because I think of you everyday

Take me away

Because of the way you feel

Take me away

Because together we are a big deal

Take me away

Because that is where I wanna go

Take me away

Where no one else will know

Tale of the Sexes

I don't sell dreams, I make them

So if you here for a reason, let me know

If you can't explain yourself,

It's best you go

Don't waste my time;

I won't waste yours

One thing is for sure; I am not into whores

So save yourself a trip

Go entertain someone else until they slip

Because I don't fall for silly tricks

And I am not your future lottery pick

Open your mind

While closing your legs

I am not about to beg

For no pussy

Cause if that is your bargaining tool

Then girl you played yourself for a fool

Maybe to some loser or some chump

You can let him thump

Get him around your finger

And use him with some strings

But at the end of the day

That don't mean you going to end up with a ring

You'll be singing the same song

Men ain't shit

He'll be singing another song

I just fuck that bitch

Tears of A Torn Heart

The greatest story I ever wrote
I will step back and let my thoughts float
I was at a point where I couldn't cope
With the pain of love
Destined at one point
For a wife, a house, and kids
But the pain of my past
Put a lid on that
If I seen love
I chased it away with a bat
Get away, Get away
No longer welcome here
I had finally realized my deepest fear
It wasn't love
But the inadequate feeling
Of loving more than you got back
Finally opening the door
Only to be met by a punch
So I found a shell
Made a home
Grew thick skin
Lived alone
The door was locked
So no one could enter
My heart was colder than the coldest winter
Tears of my torn heart
Bleed like a flowing river

I am lifeless

Not even a shiver

The greatest story I ever wrote

Because this is the end

Now I must drift in this sinking boat

Drowning because

I never found a way to cope with

Tears of a torn heart

The Big Mistake

The big mistake was opening my heart;
The most painful result was it being broken.
The biggest mistake was giving love a chance;
The hardest lesson came with the biggest cost.
The pain from within has stripped me raw,
The mistakes of others
Have taught me well.
Even if the pain burn like hell,
How do you recover from a catastrophe?
Well after every major disaster
Comes a chance to rebuild
To start over, to even heal
So the biggest mistake
Gave me the best chance
At destroying the old me since it was so damaged
Rebuilding from the mistakes of the past
To live for the present
So my future can last.

The Bitch Never Loved Me

The bitch never loved me
She had my heart,
And I thought she loved me
She played it very well
I thought we had love, but it was just the gates of hell
The bitch was good
I got to give her that
I missed the signs
That sneaky little hood rat
The bitch never loved me
Just played with my heart
Led me directly to darkness
That there is no light in sight
I loved that bitch
Now I am wondering how
I gave her my all
Yet, she turned out to be so foul
The bitch never loved me
And now I know that is fine
I just have to get back to mine
The bitch never loved me
I should be mad
I am going to look at the stars
Find a new way to be glad
The bitch never loved me
And I can't even be sad

The Difference

Drowning in a sea of tears

Trapped by the walls of my own fears

Self-inflicted from scars I wouldn't allow to heal

Dark clouds follow me as if they are my shadow

Fighting this war

Engaged in battles

With myself

Abusing my own existence

Until I ceased to exist

Struggle to hold on to this crumbling smile

Traveling this road alone

As if this is my Green Mile

Seek and Search

For a place they call bliss

Callused hands

Blistered feet

My heart is dead

No longer having a beat

Come dance with me

If you may

If you love me

Please stay

Find a place

Somewhere in my heart

Plant a seed

Cut down the weeds

Release my soul

Hold me tight

Absorb these tears

So I shall never drown again

Be the wind beneath my wings

So we can fly away

If you love me

Here you must stay

I love you

So please don't go away

The Impact

The journey was bleak;

Long days, countless nights of no sleep

Afraid to cry

(That makes a man weak)

Determine

Demanding

Strong and Standing

The impact

Of the pain

Has washed those attributes away

Now, as night turns into day

I have lost my way

The only thing following me is my shadow

And the darkness of the pain

The impact

I, stuck with the blame

Why him?

Why not me?

The impact

Like that of a ten-ton wall that has just fallen on my heart

Carted off to a pit of fire

You cut my wings;

No longer am I soaring higher

Grounded for life

The impact of your lies

Silenced

'Cause no one listens

When a man cries

The impact of the pain

With a river of sorrow

With no shoulder to borrow

The impact of your lies

The Journey

Give me a chance
And I'll prove your critics wrong,
I'll give you the beat; you got the song
I am the lock, and you are my key
So unlock my soul
While we stroll the beach
Keep walking until our destination is in sight
When I am with you, things just feel right
Sometimes afraid of what this could really be,
Coming to terms of scars from the past
I can't look back
Or this may never last
Give me some time
To make this thing right,
I won't leave you
This is worth a fight
See this thing through,
And let's gaze in the sky
A day without you
Is like a day without breath
Come back to me
I haven't been the same since you left.

The Light Within

Your lips should burn

For how you turned my words against me

Spewing venomous words

Why are you so hateful?

You turned on me

Causing us to lose sight

Which lead to fights

The end is mighty close

We are a shadow of what we used to be

Our past as dark as our shadows

We kept looking for the light at the end of the tunnel

Never realizing the light was within each other

You were my light that literally lit up my world

Now venomous words have cast a shadow

On something so bright

If you ever see the light again

I hope you see it in me

And if you regain your sight

I hope your eyes will only be for me

The Love Curse

We are together

Yet so far apart

We love each other

But is it really from the heart

We laugh and play

But our thoughts drift us away

Having late conversations

That is full of empty words

Afraid of past

Because it haunts us like our shadow

Afraid to love again

We both lost that battle

Staring into each other eyes

Hoping to find an answer

Where do lost souls go?

When they have no home

Do they wonder away forever?

Never to be seen

The funny things love does

When it wants to be mean

Love unconditional

That's what I heard

If you ask me

Love is cruel

That Shit is for the birds

The Problem with Love 2

The problem with love is we seek it
The answer is to give it.
The problem with love is we try to possess it
The answer is to honor it.
The problem with love is we need it
The answer is to let it.
The problem with love is that it hurts
The answer is to not fight back.
The problem with love is that it is pain
The answer is no pain, no gain.
The problem with love is all want to teach it
The answer is to learn it.
The problem with love is we ask why
The answer is when, where and how.
The problem with love is…there is no problem
The answer is to all our problems is love.

The Proposal

Marry my mind

Engage my soul

Hold my feelings

Caress my thoughts

Hear my words

Listen to my heart

Open these doors

That have been closed for so long

Strive for growth

Work with me

Not against me

This proposal

Is an agreement

Amongst us both

One written on flesh

Carved with stone

Soften with tears

Signed in Blood

This is my Proposal

Attached with love

The Zone

They say nice guys don't finish last
And I think it's true,
They're falling into the Friend Zone
Disappearing like shadows in the dark,
They reappear when you have a broken heart;
They know your wants, your needs, and even your dreams,
They give you a shoulder when you're crying a stream
Once the wound is healed and you've regained your strength
You take him and keep him at arm's length
Close enough to touch, but far from your heart
Once the next man breaks your spirit
You will call upon your hero
Dragging him away from the zone
Talking to him for hours, making magic on the phone
Yet, here comes another heartbreaker and you know it's true
I am fine taking this risk
As long as I got you
Mr. Friend Zone

Things I Left Behind

Years ago, I lost myself
As I travelled the road of life
I left a few things behind:
I left my heart
Thought it was with me, but it was just the weight of my pain;
The stitches had been removed, but the wound never healed correctly
Because it never healed correct it left a hole in my heart,
As I advanced in life, pieces of my heart seeped away
The things I left behind, were the pieces of my heart
Scar tissue from my soul
Memories of good times
Friends who had turned cold
The things I left, I can never get back
So I will take what I have left after the storm
Start collecting new pieces
Until I can patch together
The things I left behind.

Time with a Broken Heart

They say that times heals a broken heart

But how much time

Because time never stops

And does it end when my life ends

How do you fix something when you don't have the instructions on how to put it back together?

How does a broken heart heal when the ones trying to mend it only cause more damage?

So I have decided to not let anyone close enough to me

I'd rather walk away sometimes without even saying goodbye

With my back to those who hurt me

They won't see me cry

I can keep hiding behind this broken heart

Telling all these little lies

Because I know that time will catch up with me

Bring about all the pain of the past

I thought if I kept running and trying to hide

I could out ride this broken heart

But it keeps reappearing in different shades, different forms, and always scares as a storm

Forcing me to hold on to myself just to keep warm

I warn you to never get too close to me because the cold in my heart

Will cause frostbite

I warn you to never underestimate me because the fire in my soul

Will cause you to get burned

I tried love; it was a lessoned well-learned.

Tick Tock

My heart stopped

When I looked into your eyes

Tick tick

Because I know you're the bomb

And I don't even know you

Ready to be the fire to your fuse

So we can both be amused

Schooling each other as we escape into another world

Interaction, intertwined, and engaged

Until I can give you the engagement ring

So your heart can sing

Tick tick tick

Time is of the essence

Just like your beauty

I know you're the bomb

And I can't wait until our worlds collide

Interaction, intertwined, and engaged

To my Past Love

Sorry for the heartache
Sorry for the pain
I was focused on other things
I now realize I left you out in the rain
I thought I was gaining everything
When I was actually losing it all
Now time has past
And so has my heart
It stopped beating the second we parted
Now I don't know where to start
Because I forgot how we ended
Now I am winded
Out of breath and lost amongst my own misery
Grant me one last wish
Please if you may
Come back home
This time promise me you won't walk away
Past Love
I thought it was me that was to blame
But you were so good
I got caught in your games
Lost myself, imprisoned my mind
Closed my heart
Locked away my soul
It wasn't rain
Those were my tears
Trying to replenish my heart

While shedding away my fears

But you scared me lifeless

When I attached to your heart

You bled mine dry

Gained new life

And decided to depart

Dear Past Love

I am still alive

If you try to return

I have one unpleasant surprise

I can see right through your deceit and lies

My heart is pure

It just took loving myself first

To realize

To Watch Us This Way

Do I got to change who I am
To be the star in your eye
When I would die, just to give you life?
What burns is the view you see me as
You said you would love me,
You said you would care for me,
You said you would give to me,
But all you have given me is broken promises
That have lead me to a broken heart
Confused me so much
I can't restart
If I change, let me do the changing
I'll only change for the better
I am resilient; I'll make it through the treacherous weather
Stand by my side
Or fall by my wayside
Allowing all we could have built to wash away
But forcing me to change is not the right way
Let's open each other doors
And find a way to stay
So we can allow love to enter
Each and every day.

To Whom It May Concern

To Whom It May Concern:

This is no cry for help, but a roar for acknowledgement. As I have travelled a long, dreary road since the days of departing from my Heaven and Hell relationship. All I ask is for your tender love and care. Showing me that all women are not blood-sucking demons forcing me to pull out my hair. This is no I hate you letter, or everyone sucks. But a way to express myself, and to heal all these cuts. These self-inflicted wounds have so many scars; I think it would be less pain if I was hit by six cars. I have travelled so far, yet still have so far to go. I may fall off course, but always find my way home. Loan me a shoulder, 'cause the journey is not easy. Clean off my tears, my hands are still greasy. I am blinded by own pain, afraid of my own shame. Am I hiding from the past or afraid to get past my own demons? Fighting a battle in the dark, with no way out. Trapped in home of misery, drowning in my own sorrow, I look for the future but there seems to be no tomorrow. Trying to regain the lust that once allowed me to love, asking for help from the man above. Not knowing what is right, so it seems everything I do is wrong; trying to find a place I can finally call my home. If it's in your heart, I will rest in your soul, but just a simple reminder, I will leave once it gets too cold. Not waiting to run away, but it's all I know, until I find love.....I really have no other place to go.

-Beat Soul

Together

From dead weight to sweet bliss

This all started with a kiss

The touch of your lips

Soothed my soul

Turn my frown around

Gave me the Crown

So I could once again be King

Now the music I hear is those of songbirds

Flowing in the wind

Give me a chance

I'll give you a ring

Produce harmony

From end to end

Dead Poet

No more

You have helped closed that door

Alive again

And ready to live

Let's partake on this journey

Side by Side

Holding hands

You are my woman

I am your man

Knowing apart we don't have it all together

We can make thru any tough weather

So let me join you

So we can be together

Too Far, Too Fast

Too far too fast
I was there for you
But you just ran
I wanted to be the man
Not just your man
Ready and prepared
You drifted too far
And too fast
I can't look away
You are more than my past
Too far too fast
Has led me to a fork in the road
Either way I go
I think will lead to a lost
I can't do this
And still face the cost
It's too far to come get you
And too fast of a change
If you promise me your heart
Then here I would remain
But too far too fast
Is the name of this game
I accept the
Blame
Shame
And here I can't remain
Too far, too fast

Too Much Life to Live

Too much life

Not to live

I gave

But no one wanted to give

So these illusions are reality

Like water in a river

The thought of love

Sometimes makes me shiver

Is it fear?

Or just plain terror

My life is mine

I will endure the stormy weather

Breaking through this yoke

Unhappiness wrapped around my throat

Until I nearly choked

Yet the fire in my soul

The passion in my eyes

Broke through the pain

Penetrate the lies

Open your heart

Release your soul

Live this life

Own this moment

As if it's the last

Too much life

Not to live

Past the Past

Toss and Turn

I toss and turn at night

My mind drifts during the day

Constantly, replaying memories of happiness

Looking in the mirror only to see reflections

Of what this could have been

Reevaluating my past, trying not to beat myself up

Caught up in a whirlwind of emotions

That always lingers like a sharp pain

Trying to regain a piece of me

That has the strength to overcome this overcast

I am tired of tossing and turning

I am seeking a rising sun

While the stars shine at night

I am waiting to lie next to you

Each and every night

Until then I'll toss and turn

While my mind drifts away during the day and night

Transfer of Emotions

It was all I wanted
It was all I needed
Uprooted by tragedy
Abused by love
Covering up the wounds of my heart
Stitching myself back together with words from my pen
Running from my emotions
As darkness became my next of kin
Soul drying up
While my body turns cold
Heart so decayed that the magnets are dark like mold
Withering away
Like night into day
I had nowhere to go
No safe place to stay
So I begin to put my pen to paper
Unleashing all that I knew
Turn my dark into sky blue
Looked to the sky
As these words began to come alive
Recharging my body that had decayed from abuse
Painted a picture with words
That led me to the truth
Learned to love again
While focusing on me
Turned my dark clouds away and let the sun shine in
So as I put these words on paper it's like a second wind

So Pen to Paper keep telling the truth

Because if you keep at it

Your potential has no roof

So take those words

And live through others

So that even when the pen runs dry

You will continue to live within others

Trapped

Trapped in a bind

Losing my mind

Got a girl that is one of a kind

But trapped with a girl I left behind

Add her to my team

Cause she used to be the woman of my dreams

If I get caught disaster will flow like a stream

Sold my heart to one girl

Rented a piece to another girl

Claim to one she is my world

Telling the other I am willing to give her the world

Trapped between two

For two different reasons

One I loved all four seasons

The other is just my kind of season

She's a little spicy

She's always kept me hot

I better cut her lose

Or my ass might get shot

Trapped between

And I can't cut the cord

Walking on eggshells

Please help me, Lord

Trail of Broken Hearts

Trail of broken hearts

Lead me to a dead end

So I cut my heart out of my chest

To sacrifice my soul so they could rest

I never meant to cause them pain

I had a devil on my back

With Heaven in my eyes

Which lead to broken hearts

Because they all were laced with white lies

I have made them suffer

So I'm looking for peace

So I can lead them to peace

They all have a piece of me

That is why I fell apart

Now that I removed my heart

I can restart and use the

Trail of Broken Hearts

To start a new path

To lead me to a new heart

Cause all that is behind me is

A Trail of Broken Hearts

Tricky Little Love

If Love is a mission
Where does it end?
If I am travelling in the right direction
How do I measure the distance I travelled?
If Love has pain
How do I measure how much I been hurt?
If their gratification in Love
Who is the one gratifying me?
Love needs two hearts to make one love
Then why am I the only one here
If Love is my friend
Why did it stab me the back?
Lied to my face
Placed me in confinement
Turned me into a basket-case
They want to put me in a straitjacket
But Love is the one that is crazy
So Love as you may
But it may come at a cost
You heart might be deep
But mess with Love
And thinking you in a dream
Wake up in cold sweats
Cause it was a nightmare
You may one day regret

Under Pressure

They say the ones who love you the most

Are the ones who hurt you most

Well if I wanted to be hurt by those I trusted

I would intentionally hurt myself

Under Pressure

To keep those who matter in my life

And remove those who I don't matter to

Searching for answers, when I am questioning everyone around me

Trying to go back to the start

When I never knew where it started at

Under Pressure to make myself a better person

When those around me only wanna see me fail

They want to trap me in their misery better known as Hell

Under Pressure to be the best I can be

When other look at me it's the worse they want to see

Images of sunny days with perfect skies

Float around my head

But they slowly die

Along with my dreams

As nightmares enter my world

Under Pressure

Trying to be better

In this cruel cruel world

Unscripted

Been exposed to so much pain

You would think I am immune to it

People thinking my life is full of rainbows

They missed the storm

They missed the turmoil from within

They see these words

But could never feel the pain in them

These words aren't crying

They are a manuscript

Because my life isn't scripted

They tattooed on my brain

And my cranium needs a release

So these words are an escape

Been exposed to so much pain

You would think I am immune

Surely not the case

I listen to the same song

But I just hear a different tune

Sitting in the same room

But you can't fathom my views

Walking Away

Walking away from everything I have built

Setting it on fire

So the memories can burn with it

Never wanting to recall this difficult segment of my life

I know it taught me lessons

If I burn away the memories

I can kill my attempt at a confession

Walking Away, like it never existed

You were my heart, sunshine, and my soul

I am walking away, because this shit is old

Dead like my heart has become

Walking away even though I am numb

Crawling until I can walk again

The problem is you were a sin

Never again will I allow this type of torture

Walking away

Seems so hard

Yet, it will never be as hard as you made my life

As I walk away

Wanting Something That Doesn't Want You Back

She is on my mind

Like blood in my veins

The thought of losing her

Is driving me insane

How do you obtain something?

That doesn't want to be obtain

How do you pursue love?

When it is causing so much pain

When thoughts of happiness

Are all that remain

And all you are left with is fragments of your heart

Shredded fibers of your heart

What do you do when you want something

That doesn't want you back?

Do you keep running towards it or retreat

And never look back

Wanting something

That many never want you back

We Have so Many Problems

We have so many problems

That we can't fix with conversation

So let me take your hand

You see I am the man; you just met me as a boy

I've grown and see the growth

But you keep looking at the wounds

It consumed the best of us

Exposed the worse

But we grow from birth

So let's seize this monster

And take those problems

And create bliss

I only have one thing on my list

That's being with you

So let's not talk

Just let me do

My love for you is true and a lifetime of memories

Means nothing if I don't make them with you

We Said Goodbye with Words

We said goodbye with words

But not with our hearts

We tried to move on

But could never start anything with someone else

We said those words but what did they mean?

When every fiber of our body

Had been intertwined

Our minds always on each other's

We said goodbye with words

But not with our hearts

We remain together

When we only say goodbye with words

We Were Close Friends

We were close friends

At times even lovers

But, the love seems to have evaporated

It has evacuated our hearts

We were close friends

Once joined as one

Now it's like we are just strangers in a strange place

Under extraordinary circumstances

Faced with questions, that we fear the answers

Once close friends

Now we have closed doors

And neither of us has the courage to reopen it

We were close friends

At times even lovers

Now we're two lost loves

In a strange place like two strangers

What is Truth?

Is there truth in your touch?

Soothing in your eyes?

Do you really want to comfort me when you see tears in my eyes?

Are you telling me the truth?

Or are they subtle lies?

What is the truth?

If they are intertwined with lies

They become dirty little truths

Which lead to tears in other's eyes.

You asked me to hold on strong

Even when things are wrong

You are here

Yet, you will not hear

I held you heart close to me

Even when Love I feared

What is the truth?

When it's laced with lies

Just a rainforest of tears

With shadows of fear

What is truth?

When it's laced with lies

Just a trail of tears

With fears of a broken heart

244

What Can I Do?

What can I do

When the only person I can blame is myself

I still working on being a better man

Giving you my hand

Is the first step

To mend the wounds

I know the consequences were detrimental

To a happy ending

But I don't want this to end

This is a new beginning

The only thing that matters is you

So what can I do to rewrite the wrong

How can I change the tune

How can I prove to you I'll give you the moon

You are more than my sunshine

It was your light that removed me from the shadows

What can I do?

To have you

When a Man Loves a Woman

When a Man loves a Woman
You just know
Your heart skips a beat
With just the thought of her
The simple gaze in her eyes
Is more priceless then a first place prize
You have the prize
And this you finally realize
Your smiles
Just glow
When a man
Has found that missing piece to his heart
All that once was dark
Is no longer of worry
You found Love
So all the other things
Are petty
You have an agreement with your heart
That you are finally ready
So take her hand
And together
Weather the storms
That may lie ahead
When a Man loves a woman
He will do it
Until his heart
Is no longer red

Lifeless

And

Dead

When a Man Loves a Woman

When I Close my Eyes

When I close my eyes
I see you
When I close my eyes
I open my heart
The beauty flows
The walls disappear
My fear is eliminated
As I feel you near
You are my all
We conquer and never fall
This feeling is awe
When I close my eyes
Yet, when they open
It all disappears
My fears return
My walls have risen
My heart is closed
You are no longer near
So I close my eyes
And you'll reappear
This is only a dream
So I must hold it dear
When I close my eyes

When I say Goodbye

We tend to forget those who are important to us

We get so self-consumed that we forget others in the room

We tend to think that we are the only ones who exist

What happens when the person erases you from their most important list

When we look back, and the footprints of the person that cared about you when you
were weak, begins to fade from the waves of the ocean

When you send that text and all you receive is a faceless emotion

When the phone calls used to pile in and now they see the call and all they do
is hit end

When you use to be held in such high regards, now you are being disregarded

When all was right, and you could only see wrong

When you reach out, and all you get is a sad song

Open your mind, before they close the doors

You stuck on battles, when you should focus on the wars

How can you heal the wounds, when you keep picking at the scabs?

Why would you give up, on all that you had?

Listen to the words, before you speak

Take a leap of faith

Or put this love we have to sleep

When Nothing is Left

When the tears no longer cover up the pain

When the only person to blame is you

When no matter the brightest of the sun you remain blue

When words are not enough to absorb the hurt

When actions remind you of mimes

When the clock ticks, but no time moves

When you used to feel

When your emotions spoke loud

When you were in love and proud

When the truck of despair hit you like a meteor shower

You counted minutes as if they were hours

Now your worn down soul

Is beaten to hamburger meat

Your feet calloused from walking that mystery trail

Your new life is a written in blood signed by Hell

When you no longer care

And life is full of despair

Look in the mirror

Stare your old soul down

Find the power to turn yourself around

Learn that love has pain

Love has pleasure

But you come out stronger

If you can endure the stormy weather

So let the elements

Rain down on your parade

Yet, reemerge with passion not rage

Keep climbing that hill

Because the view from the top

No one can steal

Whispering Tears

The words are on the paper
The pen is finally dry
Yet these tears I still cry

They were suppose to heal
They were supposed to ease my soul
But yet I am still cold

Frozen from my heart out
I know the cause a Love drought
Shivering cold, left to die

I shed these tears
Why does no one hear my cry?
These tears I shed turn into ice cubes as they leave my eyes

All I can hear is the whispers of Goodbyes
Count my blessing
As I kneel to the sky

As the words on the paper fade away
So will the thought
That my tears washed away

Whispers in the Dark

I hear whispers in the dark

I am too busy trying to hide

I left so many scars on so many hearts

That I decided to become a ghost

The damage I caused was only an inkling

Of the scars on my heart

So I'll wait around for regret no more

I want to know who you think you are

When you want to whisper about love in the dark

You come around exposing my scars

Damaging an already broken heart

I can't take any more steps forward

Because of the pain behind

I am going to continue to hide behind this broken heart

As I hear those whispers in the dark

Who?

All things grow with love

Then why do I feel so small

Why do I feel my intentions have failed

How do I strive for Heaven

When my love life is Hell

Who can I tell my anguish and pain to

Without feeling ashamed

How do I become better, when I feel I am the blame

How do I seek redemption

When I've cashed in all my chips

If all things grow with love

Then why do I feel so small

Who can water this seed

To see if it can still grow

Who can I turn to

Other than God

I feel I just don't know

How do I strive for Heaven

When my love life is Hell

Who Broke My Heart?

Who broke your heart, they ask?

Well I hope you got time, 'cause that story is a task.

The better question is who didn't break it?

Built up, only to be let down

My heart was a heavyweight going pound for pound

Just like a boxer, they can only take so much

One day, they will get that fatal punch

Heart no longer beats; cause it swings at my feet

I am afraid to admit defeat

Who broke my heart, you really want to know?

Look in the mirror, there they go

Not just one, but oh so many

I would be rich if they all was worth a penny

Who broke my heart?

If you have a lifetime

Here is the list

Are you ready to start?

At the end

Will I be adding you to the list?

Of who broke my heart.

Who do I Choose?

I know either way I'll lose

I have to choose

The choice isn't easy

She has my heart

The other has my attention

Do I hold on to what I had

Or look forward to this new beginning

Either way I feel I am not winning

Caught between the past and the future

In the gutter of the present

In the presence of two amazing woman

Knowing I'll either hurt one

Or lose both

I wish there was hope

For an amicable ending

But the end is over

Before it even started

One has my heart

The other has my attention

Yet, none of us will come out this a winner

I know either way I am losing

Why Am I Scared?

What is it about love that I fear?

Is it the chance of being hurt?

What is it about love that eludes me?

Is it that I will never find it again?

Why is love painful?

Is it because the only way to feel pleasure is to endure the pain?

Why isn't love easy?

Is it because we are truly afraid to give up our broken heart?

Why must love fight me, if I am willing to surrender to it?

Is it because love won't give me a second chance

Why am I scared?

Because love is fearless

And I fear what it can do to me again.

Why Did I Love Her So Much?

Why did I love her so much?

Because I seen my present and my future in her eyes

Every moment with her erased darkness from my past

Lights became brighter

My smile grew bigger

She triggered an emotion I hadn't felt

So strong it brought me to my knees

Please let this be real

I can't take any more pain

Please let me be, if this only a test

I have one heartbeat left

And I saved it for her

So I can die in her arms

And finally feel what forever is

As I lay in her arms for eternity

This is why I loved her so much

Why Does She Cry?

Why does she cry?

Because she replies with the lies, she heard all her life

From family to friends to lovers

She blames herself for all her pain

She sheltered her heart

Because she was ashamed

She cried because she had lost all hope and trust

She wanted to believe but infused with so much doubt

Why does she cry?

Because she realized that the first lie that was ever told

Was from her own heart

When she told herself, she wasn't beautiful

And no man could ever convince her otherwise

Cause she couldn't even see it with her own two eyes

This is why she cried

She was the source of all the lies

She has ever told

Until she sees her beauty

She can never be made whole

Will This Ever Last?

Will this ever last?

I am here, but you reek of the past

What do you see?

Is it my past, or the present me?

We are perfect

But we are perfect for each other

I want you to birth my kids

You will be an amazing mother

Will this ever last?

I ask, because only you know

I am here for the long haul

I have no other place I want to go

Give this a chance

Look pass the past

I want to turn this into forever

Together we can make this last

Stop looking back

That is why it is called the past

Look at the present

This can really last

Embrace for the future

Turning this into forever

Because forever will always last

I want us together

The question is

Will this ever last?

Windows and Doors

We met and you couldn't see anything

My doors were closed, my windows covered

But I stood at the window to give you a glimpse of my soul

I let you watch to see if one day this could be your home

We sat and watched each other through the window

You put your hand up to mine

But things just weren't right

So I decided to open the door

I stood there waiting for you to come

The winds blew leaving me cold and

Wreaking havoc on what could have been our home

If you had just left the window

And entered the door

I wouldn't be here waiting all alone

Windows and Doors.

Within and Without

Love is within reach,

Yet I am without it;

I was within the standards it takes to be in love,

Yet I have been without it for so long

Within and without

Wondering if I am going to be in or out

I am so out of touch

Yet so intrigued,

Wondering if being in love is out of my league

Within and without

Can be so close or so far,

I installed bars around my heart

With no clue how to remove them

I think my heart found a new home,

Yet never told me its location

So I have been a long heartless vacation

Trying to get back to work

Has been my new mission

Looking for my heart

So I can have love in my vision

Within and without

Is so close yet so far

I can almost touch it

But it's out of reach

It just seems so far

Within the reach of love

But still without love

Within and without

Without Sensation

Heart so numb, that I can't feel your touch

Soul like a rose, beautiful yet dangerous if mishandled

Ready to endure, but my mind unsure

Love has twisted my mind, body and soul

Frozen by the cold of those that say they are my friends

I think the dream of love has reached its end

Crying tears that dry upon their release

If it wasn't for faith, I would have no peace

Heart broken into pieces

With no one to repair

Looking at myself

With nothing but a blank stare

Cling to threads that once held my heart together

It's rough out here by myself in this torturing weather

Heartbroken, with no chance of being healed

If I could remove this numbness

I am sure it's your touch I would love to feel

If I could just turn my dream

Into the sensation

That once was real

Woman of My Dreams

Who was she?

The woman of my dreams

Or the devil in a red dress

She tested my every nerve

But she was so addictive

It was more than her aura

It was her whole being

I could see magic in her walk

I got lost in her words

She was memorizing

Who was she?

The woman of my dreams

Or the devil in a red dress

To me it didn't matter

I would dance with the devil

Just to be close to you

Hoping if she was the devil

That she would one day become my angel

The woman of my dreams

Worthless

I've loved so much

That I've become numb

Silent to kind words

Afraid of a gentle touch

I say a lot

But people don't listen much

They hear your pain

But are never here

When you need that shoulder

So you become a little harder

Jaded a little more by the minute

I've loved so much

That I've become numb

When my love was loud no one could hear

So now that it's silent, the touch is numb

And all those sweet words fall on deaf ear

So I am not afraid of your touch

I am afraid of giving my heart and being told it's not worth much

Would You?

If I confess to you

Would you want to listen?

Would you hear the sounds of my pain?

The confession of my anguish and shame

My vision, my rebound, and my triumph

Or would you trample all over my dreams

Putting blame all on me, because you said I was too blind to see

Would you meet me half way between compromise and compassion

To open up your heart and soul to my confessions

If I confess only my pain, would that be all you hear?

If I confessed my love, would you feel it?

I am here to confess

The question is; will you listen?

Here is my confession to you

I confess, I love you

Meet me half way and I'll know you love me too

You Broke My Heart

I couldn't express the pain
Yet, it was so obvious and so deep
I would lie next to you, but could never sleep
You broke my heart
I just wouldn't let you go
I walked away, but the misery controlled the show
Walking around with a broken heart
Looking for the tools to heal the wounds
I took a piece of each person I met
To sew back the missing pieces of my heart
They never fit perfectly
They just played their part
You broke my heart
So how do I fix it?
I have no clue where to start
I am no surgeon
So I can't do it on my own
I just need a safe place
I can call home
If you're not here to heal my heart
It's best you just leave me alone
You broke my heart

You Might Be Right

Maybe I dream too much

Maybe you were right

Maybe I bit the apple

And that is why I suffer

I used to enjoy the pain

It made me strong

Until I realized all I had, I lost

Assuming that it was all a gain

You might be right

Because you make me feel so wrong

I am going to the ocean, to sing my favorite song

"Let me be me"

Is all my heart will ever know

You might be right

Yet, if you don't like it

Let me show you to the door

You On My Mind

I wake up with you on my mind,

I keep thinking why we are apart.

Then I feel this feeling of being lost,

I finally realize that my action had a cost.

When I go to bed you are on my mind,

I toss and turn, wondering why we are apart.

Then I feel the feeling of hope,

I tell myself I can cope with making this work.

I wake up with you on my mind,

I keep thinking why we are apart.

Then I get this feeling of you in my life.

I finally realize that you're gone and....

I am lost without your hope, with you on my mind.

Sleepless Pen Endless Canvas

Sleepless pen endless canvas

Speak to my thoughts

They won't let me sleep

This pen meets this canvas like

Harry met Sally

While they were sleepless in Seattle

Please guide this pen

So I can end these sleepless nights

Endless is my love for this canvas

That paints the past and present of others

That the light of the future will become bright

Sleepless nights with my pen

Endless canvas in my hand

When paper meets pen

It's usually a sleepless pen on a sleepless night

With an endless canvas in hand

www.ingramcontent.com/pod-product-compliance
Lightning Source LLC
Chambersburg PA
CBHW060256100426
42742CB00011B/1771